Building Blocks

Building Blocks

Building a Parent-Child Literacy Program at Your Library

Sharon Snow

LIBRARIES UNLIMITED

A Member of the Greenwood Publishing Group

Westport, Connecticut • London

Library of Congress Cataloging-in-Publication Data

Snow, Sharon.
  Building blocks : building a parent-child literacy program at your library / Sharon Snow.
    p. cm.
  Includes bibliographical references and index.
  ISBN–13: 978–1–59158–471–1 (alk. paper)
  1. Children's libraries—Activity programs—United States. 2. Family literacy programs—United
States. 3. Reading—Parent participation—United States. 4. Language arts (Early childhood)—United
States. 5. Early childhood education—Activity programs—United States. I. Title.
  Z718.2.U6S66 2007
  027.62′5—dc22   2007007921

British Library Cataloguing in Publication Data is available.

Library of Congress Catalog Card Number: 2007007921
ISBN-13: 978–1–59158–471–1

First published in 2007   3711

Libraries Unlimited, 88 Post Road West, Westport, CT 06881
A Member of the Greenwood Publishing Group, Inc.
www.lu.com

Printed in the United States of America

∞™

The paper used in this book complies with the
Permanent Paper Standard issued by the National
Information Standards Organization (Z39.48–1984).

10 9 8 7 6 5 4 3 2 1

Contents

Appendixes

Acknowledgments

To my husband and best friend Art Snow, who has always supported and encouraged my dedication to my profession.

To my former supervisor and good friend Nora Conte, who dragged me kicking and screaming into the Reading Readiness Program. Thank you.

To my former teammates and friends, Vicki Mata, Michelle Amores, Lucia Farnham-Hudson, Claire Glennon, and Ila Langner, and the children's tutor Carmen Avila, who worked so hard to make the Reading Readiness Program a success and who was willing to take it to the California Library Association Conference in 2005.

To my editor, Blanche Woolls, who saw the presentation at the conference and had a vision that I could make the program into a book.

Introduction

Building Blocks: Building a Parent-Child Early Literacy Program at Your Library is a tool for children's librarians to use for parent-child early literacy programs. This book includes handouts and activities for six parent and child workshops featuring the six basic early literacy skills. These workshops are designed in two units, one for parents and one for children, and are presented simultaneously.

This program is made up of six components which can be presented in six or four sessions, one each week or once a month for six months. It is important that both the child and the parent attend all sessions. If six weeks does not fit into your library's schedule, it can be completed in four weeks or months, doing two skills per session.

Each session, one of the early literacy skills will be presented. Similar activities will be conducted in both the children's and parent's sections. Parents will learn the values of the six skills and activities and then they will be asked to do them at home with their child. The most important ideas that parents will take away with them is that learning can be fun. We don't teach them to teach their children to read; rather we want to give parents tools to provide their children with fun experiences that reinforce early literacy skills. A very important thing for parents to remember is that this process should be *fun* for the child *and* the parent.

Parents are a child's first teachers. They know when their child is in a good mood, which is important for learning. Children love to do things with their parents. They want to learn from them. The program will encourage parents to make time to sing, read, and play with their children. The program will also emphasize the importance of talking to their child. They need to understand that children who enter school with a large vocabulary are more likely to succeed in school.

The sessions teach parents to give their child an opportunity to explore and experience new things, and to take advantage of the many museums and other attractions in the community. Many museums have discounted admission for children with family passes and programs for low-income families. If a parent is not comfortable going to some of these locations independently, many of them have special programs for parents and children so that the family becomes accustomed to the place. In this way they and other families can learn together.

Public libraries offer a wide variety of free programs for parents and children. Children's librarians need to encourage parents to take part in as many programs as possible. This means an active promotional program with plenty of flyers placed out in the community for parents to take home.

Parents must also be encouraged to come to the library. The first assignment for the early literacy workshops is to have the parent get a library card and one for their child. They should be given an introduction to the library's Web site so they can find out about programming and other services available to them at the library.

Each week both the children and parents begin their class with the same welcoming song and the ABC song. This is important because they will both know the songs and be able sing these songs on the way walking home or driving in the car and later at home. Each week, provide as many books as possible for parents to look at and check out to take home. As each skill is introduced, corresponding books should be introduced to reinforce the skill. Children's librarians must model good read aloud skills for the parents. Reading aloud from some of the books will entice the audience to check them out to take home.

1

Libraries and Early Literacy: A Background

Librarians can stay relevant in the twenty-first century when they build on those areas where they have excelled. One of these areas is service to youth. A hot topic today is early-emergent literacy for children ages 0–6. Librarians also need to be players in the No Child Left Behind initiative and in campaigns designed to get children ready to read and ready for school.

In 1989, Elizabeth Sulzby and William H. Teale presented the idea of *emergent literacy* as reading and writing behaviors that precede conventional literacy. *Early literacy* is the earliest phases of literacy development, the period between birth and the time when children read and write conventionally.

Librarians can disseminate early literacy skills by providing four key services: programs, materials, age-appropriate spaces, and the opportunity for families, parents, and caregivers to gain skills through modeling. Libraries have always been the perfect place to nurture and foster lifelong learning with family literacy programs.

Programming

For many years, California's public libraries have included a Families for Literacy component of adult literacy programs. Families for Literacy includes three elements: literacy instruction for adults including parenting education; pre-reading and other literacy activities for children; and time for parents to use their new literacy skills with their children. The most important part happens when parents and children come together and interact with each other.

At the Dr. Robert Cruz Alum Rock Branch of the San Jose Public Library, Reading Readiness was a program in which librarians conducted reading readiness workshops for parents and, simultaneously, the children worked on their pre-reading skills. The goal was for parents to have the knowledge, skills, and activities to use in the home with their children. Their children would be learning pre-reading skills that they would be ready to do at home and would continue to strengthen while having fun learning with their parents.

Children's librarians are natural partners to help parents in the most important role they will ever take on, their child's first teacher. Librarians understand the importance of reading aloud and talking about stories help to children love books and language. However, many children's librarians need training that goes a few steps further. They need to understand early childhood development and how to incorporate pre-reading skills, such as talking to children about new and unusual words encountered in stories, asking children to predict what happened next in the story based on illustrations, and how to model these activities for parents and caregivers in their story times. The National Institute of Children's Health and Human Development (NICHD), the American Library Association (ALA), and the Public Library Association (PLA) worked together to design a program for children's librarians,

In 2000, the NICHD and PLA came together to create the Preschool Literacy Initiative. The project is designed:

- to link reading research into action,
- to get the word out to parents and caregivers that learning to read is not instinctual; but must be taught, and
- to assess the ability of librarians and libraries to effect the desired change.

ALA's Association for Library Services to Children (ALSC) joined in the effort in 2001 to create accompanying project materials and to form a joint division task force with the ALA and PLA. Children's librarians at 20 public libraries became demonstration sites. They changed their story times to include tips for parents and caregivers on how to actively participate in their children's literacy development.

Story time is a good the starting place. Through subtle changes in regular story times and the addition of parent education classes, librarians are introducing adults to new concepts and strategies that will help prepare children for reading.

Only a decade or less ago, many librarians excluded parents from story times. Librarians have relaxed that rule, actively encouraging parents to attend. Many librarians have begun introducing story time for different ages: babies and toddlers as well as pre-schoolers. They encourage stay and play times for parents after the program. Some librarians are beginning pre-reading workshops. Some examples of programs that have been reported from across the nation include the Multnomah County Library in Portland, Oregon and the Pasadena Public Library, Pasadena, California. In these programs, librarians present infomercials, scripted messages to parents and caregivers, suggesting ways that rhymes, games, and other language enrichment activities from story time can be introduced in the home. In the past, librarians have shied away from formally introducing the alphabet except to sing the ABC song, because they feared that it could be too much like school. Librarians have now begun introducing letter-sound relationships by sharing appropriate children's books, as well as encouraging play with felt and form letters, and reading alphabet books. The Provo (Utah) City Library Children's Service Manager, Carla Morris, says that "patrons and parents, have increased their respect and confidence in libraries and storytellers (librarians) who use and understand correct emergent-literacy terms. They are pleased to take part in story times that have substance."

Public libraries in Maryland have launched a state-wide language-development program, It's Never Too Early, that uses the latest research to help parents prepare their preschoolers for success in school. Despite the lack of empirical proof, Stephanie Shauck, a youth services consultant for the Maryland State Department of Education feels the program has accomplished one essential thing: public librarians are learning the lingo of educational terms such as "assessment" and "indicators." This has given them an entrée into schools, and now Maryland's public librarians are being taken seriously as partners in children's education.

Materials

Chicago's Get Wild about Reading program has expanded the Chicago library system's picture book collection, pre-primers, and phonics text, and librarians have developed ABC Backpacks for parents to check out. These backpacks include books, activities, and educational toys. Another popular program encourages parents and caregivers to read to their children. Parents sign a pledge to read aloud twenty minutes a day to their children and receive a baseball cap that says "Designated Reader." Bernadette Nowakowski, Director of Children's and Young Adult Services in Chicago, says, "We are trying to create a culture of reading and have to start with the very young."[1] Sometimes this culture requires a change in spaces.

Age-Appropriate Spaces

In 1996, Libraries for the Future, a national library advocacy organization, formed a partnership with Middle County Public Library in Centereach, New York, in order to create a model for meeting the needs of library services for young children. Family Place Libraries believe that literacy begins at birth and libraries can help build healthy communities by nourishing families. The libraries create a space where young children and their caregivers can play and learn together. Parent/Child workshops are held that feature books, toys, art supplies and professionals from community agencies who can answer caregivers questions about their children.

As library services to children change, children's spaces in the library are also evolving. Play is a child's work and primary activity and a means by which emergent literacy is fostered. Children's librarians can incorporate play into their early childhood offerings through the design of the children's space. The design of children's space and furnishings can help give parents the opportunity to play with their children in an environment that models play supporting learning. Emergent literacy is the assemblage of skills young children accumulate through hands-on, age-appropriate play experiences, involving listening, speaking, being read to, handling books, and using writing implements before they are ready for reading and writing instruction.

Carroll County Public Library in Maryland has created a Library Discovery Zone, an area designed to attract at-risk parents and their children. The zone is bright and colorful and offers computers with learning games and software. These zones are staffed with personnel who have been trained to make sure using the library is a pleasant experience for parents and their children.

Another library that has a changed the look of their children's area is West Bloomfield, Minnesota. The Youth Services Portal at the Main Library features activities that are designed to facilitate learning across all developmental skills: language and literacy, gross and fine motor, creativity, problem solving, and sensory stimulation. A Whisper

Tube is used to communicate with someone in another part of the room. It is a great tool for fostering narrative skills and stimulating the sense of hearing. Signage throughout the youth department educates parents on the importance of learning in the early years. All activities featured in the youth department aim to foster active learning and meaningful interaction between parent and child. The Westacres Branch also has an Activity Center dedicated solely to creative play and learning. For more information please go to http://www.wbib.org/virtualtour/youthportalexit.htm.

Opportunities for Families, Parents, and Caregivers

Librarians have learned that to reach families, the families must feel comfortable in the library and make the library part of their family culture. Many potential users are not aware of the free opportunities available at libraries. Children's librarians are reaching out to community organizations to form partnerships in order to reach these families. Baltimore County Public children's librarians did something that wasn't easy. They made cold calls to every agency in the county that had anything to do with birth and parenting. These calls were very successful. Now they have Baby Boosters, traveling librarians, who go to infant-toddler programs, mom's groups, PTA's prenatal classes, and postpartum support groups at local hospitals. They share the results of recent cognitive brain research and demonstrate how reading, rhyming, and singing can stimulate language centers of the developing brain. Since December 2000, they have reached 12,000 children and their parents.

Parent-Child Home Program (http://www.parent-child.org/htm) train home visitors in how to introduce age-appropriate toys and books to parents and young children. This bypasses the barrier of getting to the library. Home visitors come to the families and encourage increased parent-child verbal interaction through gentle modeling of play and reading activities. Once they have developed a relationship with parents and children, they encourage visits to the library to gain exposure to additional resources, services, and play techniques.

Libraries have always been the perfect place to nurture and foster lifelong learning. Now they are the perfect place for families with young children to come to share books and learn parenting skills. Books and play are natural partners to help parents in the most important role they will ever assume, providing a nurturing and stimulating environment for their children. Children's librarians need to ask what they can do with the materials, space, and funds available to make the library a place that promotes and models early-emergent literacy.

A very important component is the program suggested in this book, parent-child workshops that teach parents and children pre-reading skills. Advertising is important to attract participants for your workshop. A flyer and a letter to parents are shown below. You may use these as models.

Reading
Readiness Program*

*For children ages 3 ½ to 5 years
and their parents.*

The Reading Readiness program will assist children in developing early literacy skills.

Parents will also participate in workshops and learn about the six early literacy skills their children need to learn to read.

Saturdays, May 7 through May 28

9:00 – 11:30 A.M.

at the

Put your Library's Name here:

*Spaces are limited and pre-registration is required.

Please call
(*put your library's information and logo here.*)

Your Library Name
Address
City, State Zip
Telephone number

Dear Parents:

We are so glad that you and your child (children)are joining the **Reading Readiness Program**. We enjoy offering this program and you will learn how to help your child to become a life long reader.

Here are a few suggestions so you and your child (children) will get the most out of this program:

- Eat a good and nourishing breakfast. This is the most important meal of the day and prepares you and your child for fun and learning.

- Please arrive at least l5 minutes before the workshops start. The workshops start at 9:30 A.M. sharp and end at 11:00 A.M. (with the exception of the last workshop on October 15). This allows you enough time to check in, and say good-bye to your child. You will have an opportunity to observe your child during the program if you wish.

- Please take your child to the bathroom before the workshop starts.

- Toys and snacks are not allowed in the learning area.

This is a six-week program and we ask you to please attend all workshops. The sixth week or the last workshop is 2 hours (9:30 -11:30 A.M.) so that we can celebrate your successes and congratulate you and your child for learning together.

To arrange for an accommodation under the American with Disabilities Act, please call (your telephone number) TTY at least 48 hours prior to the event.

From *Building Blocks: Building a Parent-Child Early Literacy Program at Your Library* by Sharon Snow. Westport, CT: Libraries Unlimited. Copyright © 2007 by Sharon Snow.

The remainder of the book provides instructions for a series of six workshops with sessions outlined for parents' as well as those for children's sessions. The next chapter begins with a general discussion on how to plan the workshops.

Note

1. Bernadette Nowakowski (Director of Children's and Young Adult Services), in discussion with the author, DATE.

2

Introduction to the Workshops

This series of workshops, Building Blocks, presents six early literacy skills (print motivation, print awareness, letter knowledge, vocabulary, narrative, and phonological awareness) to parents and their children simultaneously. The literacy skills parents learn during their workshop will enable them to reinforce what their children learn with their librarian in their session.

The components for this program can be presented in a series of six sessions. It is important that both the child and parent attend all sessions whether you present them weekly or monthly. Because it might be more difficult to get commitments over a longer period of time, these workshops can also be presented in four weeks by combining the skills. A celebration is a fun way to end the program, so you might want to have the last week's session last two hours.

The Building Blocks program requires a great deal of help. It will be unlikely that sufficient staff could be assigned the days of the workshops. This is a good place to use volunteers and high school students who are doing service credit. It is a fun and interesting assignment for anyone.

Many components of the workshops are repeated each week. In this chapter we will learn about the general components of the program, why parents must be involved in their children's early experiences, and what they will be doing when they return home. These are the parts of the program which will be repeated at each session with additional activities given related to the specific early literacy skill. The children's workshops parallel the adult workshops, and many activities and books are used in both workshops. This allows the child and the parent to know the same songs, finger plays, and activities. Some of the activities in the children's workshops are best done in a groups setting. Parents will be given additional activities that are better done one-on-one.

Some general information is provided below. It is information that parents must learn, and you must decide how much of it you will repeat each session.

General Preparation for the Workshops

General preparations for the workshops are the same for each session. If something different is needed for a particular workshop, it will be stated for that session.

It is best to have a separate room for workshops. If this is not possible, try to find the most secluded areas in the library. You will need two areas, one for parents and one for children. It needs to be an area where others will not be intruding, you won't be disturbing others, and the participants will not be distracted.

If the library is too small for this, partner with another agency to use their facility. This partnership could be a preschool, community center, or another facility. Use what you have. The challenge with using another facility is that the parents and the children are not able to see and enjoy the library setting, so, if this happens, include a field trip to the library in the program. To accommodate this you may have to extend one week's program by half an hour to an hour. It is important that the parents and children to be familiar with the library and to be comfortable going to the library.

Another inconvenience is that all the materials must be taken to the facility, unless it is a childcare facility where you might be able to use some of their materials. The time to set up and clean up will also be expanded.

A checklist to help you prepare for your sessions is shown below:

Weekly Checklist

Checklist for Each Week's Program

Setup for the Children's Workshop (At Least One Day in Advance)

1. Decorate room with educational materials (e.g., posters, rhymes, pictures) to be child friendly, if possible. Check to see if you have the following supplies: crayons, colored paper, scissors, glue sticks, old magazines and newspapers, covering for craft tables (heavy craft paper, newspaper, or plastic tablecloths), cleaning wipes, and tissues.
2. Prepare a folder for each child.
   The folder should have plastic paper protectors for the child's paperwork. Each week, keep the worksheets and craft projects and put them in the folder at the end of the workshop. The folders will be presented to the children and parent at the celebration as a reminder of the work that they have accomplished.
3. On a table place a sign-in sheet for parents.
   You will need name tags for parents and children. You should try to find name tag lanyards with a plastic pocket to insert the name tag for both. These are excellent to use because stick-on name tags are too easy for children to pull off, and you don't have to worry about pins to pin on tags. Also, the lanyards are reusable. One source for these is Lakeshore Learning Materials. You will be placing the child's name with the parents' name below for the children and the reverse for the parents.
4. Set up a felt board and felt letters, a magnetic board with magnetic alphabet letters, a basket full of books to read, puppets, blocks and other toys, worksheets, and craft supplies.
5. Prepare an area where children can play with the felt and magnetic letters, look at books and puppets, and can sit at tables for doing craft and writing projects.

Setup for the Parents' Area (Can Be Done an Hour before Program Starts)

1. Make coffee (optional)
2. Lay out pre-prepared handouts, notepaper and pencils, any craft materials for the day or samples of craft projects.
3. Prepare and set out a suggestion box for further questions and suggestions. This is optional and can be used instead of or in addition to an evaluation form.
4. Bring out the books to choose from at end of the program, from the Picture Books Everyone Should Know bibliography (see Appendix A).
   Keep one cart for your demo books, and one for the parents to use. If you are in a system that has multiple copies of titles or are able to borrow from another library, have extra copies of some of the most popular titles. You want to be able to have enough books for parents to have a good selection of books to check out. If funds are available order extra titles.
5. In order to start on time, make the area accessible at least fifteen minutes ahead of time.

Choosing and Recording Your Books, Songs, and Finger Plays

Repetition is important. Children like to hear the same stories and finger plays repeatedly. Rereading the familiar reinforces how children learn. Repetition improves vocabulary, sequencing, and memory skills. Each reading brings a little more meaning to the story. It is very important that the same songs are sung, and the same finger plays are taught. Plan which songs and finger plays you will use before you begin your workshops. It is also a good idea to plan ahead for which the books you will talk about. The chart of Materials to Be Used can help you to organize your books, songs, and finger plays. Some of the suggestions from the workshops have been added here as examples.

Table 2.1
Materials to Be Used

Week	Books	Songs	Finger Plays	Activity
Each		Welcoming Song ABC Song Closing Song		Shake the Sillies
1	Chicka Chicka Boom Boom			
2				
3		My Bonnie Lies over the Ocean		
4	Napping House	Down by the Bay	Itsy Bitsy Spider	

The finger plays are suggestions and you may want to change some of the finger plays and songs to those that you already use in your programs or to those that you are more familiar with. The bibliographies are suggested materials and can be changed to those that are available in your library, newer titles, or reflect the interest and needs of your community.

Parents should be encouraged to arrive fifteen minutes prior to the starting time of the workshops. This allows the parents time to sign in, spend a couple of minutes getting their child settled in, and maybe taking a minute or two to look at a book or check out the puppets or other toys. They need to let their child know that they are going to their class and will see them at the end of the program. Having them arrive early allows the workshop to start promptly at the scheduled time.

Table 2.2
Attendance: 10/30/20–Reading Readiness Workshop Sign-in Sheet

	Child's Name	Parent's Name	Time In	Signature	Time Out	Signature
1						
2						
3						
4						
5						
6						
7						
8						
9						
10						
11						
12						
13						
14						
15						
16						
17						
18						
19						
20						

When the parent and child arrive, two greeters are available to help parents sign in and make name tags for themselves and their child. A sample sign-in sheet is shown on the previous page.

Parents now say good-bye to their child and head to the parent workshop in another room or area. Children are encouraged to look at books, or play with puppets or toys while they wait for the workshop to begin.

As the children sign in, help them put their name on a folder that will be used for their work. When an activity is completed, the child will print his name on the activity. At the end of the session these will be collected and put into the appropriate folder.

Weekly Beginning for the Children's Workshops

When children have signed in, they may gather in an activity area that has a basket of books from the bibliography, Picture Books Everyone Should Know, found in Appendix A. These should be set out for children to browse through while waiting for everyone to arrive. This allows them to make friends with books, especially if they have limited exposure to books at home, and encourages them to take books home at the end of the session. Other appropriate toys can be put out for play while waiting. Recommended items would be puppets, alphabet blocks, and other activities that promote the pre-reading skills. Parents are encouraged to stay with their children and play with them.

Promptly at the scheduled time, parents go to their workshop. Ask the children to leave all toys and books in the baskets. Have them gather together in a large circle. Introduce the staff and volunteers. Give the children a few simple rules. These rules should include: putting on their listening ears, raising their hands when they want to speak, making sure to have an adult with them if they need to leave the room or area, and making sure to tell one of the adults if they need to go to the bathroom.

After giving the children the rules, you can start the first session with getting to know each other. For example, you can say, "Good morning. My name is (what you would like to be called). Next to me is . . ." The child next to you says his or her name. Everyone then says, "Good morning, (name)." Continue around the room until all the children have said their names and heard "Good morning (name)."

Because each workshop continues with the same opening song, you should choose a song that you enjoy. Some possibilities for beginning songs are shown in Appendix B. Letter knowledge activities will be presented at each of the workshops, as this is one of the most important skills for pre-reading.

To end each week's workshop parents can join their children for a story time that reinforces the activities that have been presented. This reinforces the idea of doing activities together during the week. If children or parents have not chosen a book to take home to read before the next session, encourage them to do so now. Parent's will then sign their children out and return their name tags.

Weekly Beginning for the Parents' Workshop

At the first workshop, give each parent a folder for their handouts and notes. Ask them to take the folder home with them to review during the week to remind them of activities, songs and finger plays to do with their children. Also, provide paper and pen for note taking. Each workshop will begin with introduction of the staff. Then, ask parents to introduce themselves. At the second session when you ask parents to get pens and paper from their folders to make notes, some parents may have forgotten the folder. You will need to have additional paper ready for them to use.

Their first assignment is to get a library card for themselves and their child. It is important for both to have a card so that the child becomes a library patron, too. If parents have not yet signed up for a library card, remind them of the importance of having a library card. Have applications ready for them to hand to them.

Materials for craft projects can be assembled in baggies to take home for those parents who do not have such materials in the home. This is an option. Other parents will have these materials at home.

General Information for Parents

Parents will learn the values of the six skills pre-reading skills and activities that they can do at home with their child. The children will be participating in these activities in their sessions. The most important idea that parents will take away with them is that *learning can be fun.* Activities that reinforce each skill will be provided. Another important thing to remember is, we are not teaching their children to read we are giving them the skills to be ready to read. We want parents to be able to have fun with their child while getting them ready for school and reading.

Parents are a child's first teacher. They know things about their child that will help them learn. They know when their child is in a good mood, which is important for learning. Children love to do things with their parent and want to learn from them. Parents should make time to sing, read, and play with their child. Talking with their child, parents exposes their child to new words, helping children learn to communicate in complete sentences. Children who enter school with a large vocabulary are more likely to succeed in school.

Parents should be reminded that their children need opportunities to explore and experience new things, and many of these new things are outside the library. Parents can take advantage of the various venues in the community. Many museums have discounted admissions for children, family passes, and programs for low-income families. If a family is not comfortable going to some of these locations, you can point out they have many special programs that parents can take part in to get accustomed to a place. You could even have a specific one to recommend. You might suggest that they go with other families and learn together. Hopefully, the session you are presenting may offer an opportunity for parents to meet and build relationships that would allow them to attend the same program at a museum so they could have a partner to go with to a new activity.

Tell parents about the wide variety of other programs for parents and children at the library, and that these programs are free. Parents should be encouraged to take part in as many of these as possible. As new programs are offered, give parents an opportunity to take one or several flyers to take home with them. Introduce parents to the library's Web site and show them how to find the events and programs online.

You must decide how much of the above information you need to repeat to your parents during their sessions. Some parents may need more reminders than others. Each group of parents will be different, and you will need to review your weekly evaluation sheets to decide this.

Weekly Closing Activities

At the end of each session, parents rejoin their children for the closing activities such as hearing a story or singing the closing song. Encourage the parents to fill out an evaluation form or to write suggestions to put in the suggestion box. A sample form is shown below.

Give the parents a weekly assignment sheet. The assignment sheet gives added emphasis to the workshop. Assignment sheets stress the importance of continuing these activities at home. At the beginning of the next workshop, parents will tell about some of the activities and books that they have shared with their children during the week.

Remind parents to bring back their folders the next week. Also, if they do not have their library cards, they should get one so they are ready to check out books.

Specific Preparations

For each session there are materials that can be prepared for ahead of time. You will need two sets of the materials, one for the parent workshops and one for the children's workshops.

For the first session, print motivation, you will need a set of magnetic or flannel alphabet letters and pictures of objects for each letter of the alphabet. You may be able to cut these out from alphabet books you are planning to discard, coloring books, or you may find be able to download pictures from the Internet. Mount the pictures on heavy construction paper and laminate as you will be using them more than once. You will also be showing a pop-up book.

Print awareness, the second session, requires three-by-five-inch index cards, old business cards, or small pieces of paper about the size of business cards. The other items that you need for this session are pictures of signs that children might see in their neighborhood. These can include road signs. You can also take photographs or find ads for businesses they might see as they are riding in the car. Again, laminate the pictures so that they are more durable. You can also add felt or magnets to the picture in order to use on a flannel or magnetic board.

The third session, devoted to letter knowledge, will allow you to re-use pictures you have used in the first two sessions. Create a worksheet that has letters with straight lines, curved lines, and a combination of both curved and straight lines. Give the children three crayons—blue, green, and red. They will use the blue crayon to trace around the straight line letters, the green for the curved letters, and the red for the letters that are a combination of straight and curved lines. If you don't have enough crayons in these three colors for each child, they can share. Create large letters made from thin styroform, large sheets of paper, to put on the floor. Or painter's tape can be used to make the letters directly on the floor. Children are then ask to move in a variety of ways—hop, skip, jump, crawl, or run—to a letter as it is called out.

The vocabulary session requires the creation of a word box (shoe or other small box), three-by-five-inch cards, old business cards or pieces of paper, and a children's dictionary from your collection. You will also be labeling some of the objects around the room.

For the narrative workshop, you will need some plastic food, available at a school supply store in your area, a paper grocery bag or a plastic shopping basket, color sheets, lacing letters, or numbers to trace. You should try to have an example of all three to show the parents.

For the phonological session, you will need worksheets. Because you will introducing easy readers to parents, you should pull a number of these from your shelves. You will also be introducing Rylant's *Henry and Mudge and the Great Grandpas,* and you will need copies of the Hawkins and Cox series books to share with parents.

In chapter 3, the first adult workshop is outlined. Parents will be introduced to the first literacy skill, print motivation.

Reading Readiness Evaluation

Let us know what you think!

1. *I learned something that I can use with my child.   Please circle*

Strongly agree   Agree   Somewhat agree   Disagree   Strongly Disagree

2. *The information was presented in a way that I can use it. Please circle*

Strongly agree   Agree   Somewhat agree   Disagree   Strongly Disagree

3. *The best part was* _____

_____

4. *The part that needs to be improved is* _____

_____

5. *One idea that I am going to do this week with my child (children) is* _____

_____

6. *Other comments* _____

_____

We enjoyed having you in our workshop.
Thank you for giving us your ideas!

3

Print Motivation: First Session Adult Workshop

During this session, you will be introducing parents to print motivation, which is defined as developing interest in and enjoyment of books. In preparation for this workshop you will need a set of either magnetic or flannel alphabet letters and pictures representing each of these letters. As suggested in chapter 2, these pictures can be taken from worn-out alphabet books, coloring books, or the Internet.

Start this session by giving the parents a folder, some paper, and a pen. Tell them that during the program they will be receiving handouts with activities to use at home during the week with their children. They will take the folder home with them and they need to bring it back each week.

Next, make introductions, asking everyone to give their name. Ask if they read aloud to their children and if so, how often. Ask if their children have their own books, and finally, ask why the parents chose to come to the workshop.

Give them the words to the welcoming song and the ABC song (Appendix B) that you will be using. The one you use to welcome the group can be the one that you use at story time or it can be another song of your choice. Make a handout for the words so parents can sing along with you. Tell them their children will also be singing both songs.

Then sing the welcoming song and the ABC song and ask them to join in. Since this may be the first time they may have sung these songs, you might want to sing them first and then ask them to join in. Remind them that you will be using both songs during every session and that their children will also be singing those songs in their workshop. Suggest they sing it with their children on the way home. Explain that you will be introducing the songs and finger plays that their children are learning and ask that they participate with you so that they can do them with their children each week.

In your lecture, you will be making the following points:

- Children need to make friends with books. They need to be taught that books are their friends, and they need to be shown how to treat books with respect.
- The more experiences children have with language, the easier it is for them to learn to read.
- Children need to hear and join in conversations both with adults and with children.

- Parents are role models, and children love to imitate them. Therefore, it is important that they see their parents reading. Many times parents read once the children have gone to bed, and it is quiet. By turning off the television before bedtime, a parent and child can read together, and then each can read a few minutes separately. Reading together and then separately can take place at other times during the day when there is a break from the day's busy activities.
- The home should be a literary environment. Introduce parents to the Web site www.getreadytoread.org, and to the Home Literacy Environment Checklist, which is available in both Spanish and English. A partial copy of the checklist is shown in Appendix C.
- Books are available to be borrowed from the library. Public libraries are a free source of books and this allows parents to have a variety of books available in the home.

It is important to emphasize to the parents that children should also own books and have a place to keep their books. Grandparents, relatives, and friends should be encouraged to give children books as gifts.

Special books might be put on the top shelf to be looked at with Mom and Dad and handled with care. You may want to show the parents different kinds of special books, such as pop-up books, that their children may want to keep as a reminder of their childhood. However, children need not always have new books or books that they will want to keep. It is important that children need books they can use every day, anywhere. These books may be paperback as well as hardback, new or used. The important thing is that they must have books around them all the time.

You can suggest that the parents think about starting a book exchange with their children's friends as a way to get new or different books into the home. Books do not have to be kept forever. When a child has grown tired of a book or is reading more difficult books, pass those books on to friends and relatives. If they are in really good condition, see if their day care would like to have them or put them in a yard sale.

If there is a children's bookstore in town, be sure to tell parents about this store. Staff members at the bookstore are also experts who can help parents find the right book for their child. Even if there is no bookstore devoted to children's books, the commercial bookstores all have children's sections, and most have knowledgeable sales persons to help with selection.

Children need to be surrounded by books and other forms of print. Books that have moveable parts, flaps to lift, and objects that pop up will attach a child's attention. Emphasize to parents that books should be included with the toys which children play with everyday.

Children who enter school knowing how to handle a book, holding it right, and reading from left to right will have a head start in school. Children need to learn that books have a front and back, and an up and down. Then also need to know books open right to left, and that we read right to left and from top to bottom. If they start school knowing these concepts, they will have a good start on learning to read.

After this part of the program, it is a good time to introduce songs or finger plays that require the parents to stand and move around. This should mirror what is being covered in the children's workshop.

Additional suggestions for finger plays are found in Appendix B, which contains finger plays that everyone should know, and in Appendix D ("Print Awareness and Print Motivation"). You must match the activities you choose for the parents to the activities the children will also be learning during their workshop.

Give time for the parents to ask questions as you go along. Getting their input and questions makes the information more meaningful for them.

After introducing the songs and finger plays to the parents, it is then time to share book suggestions with them. You may choose books from Appendix E ("Print Motivation Bibliography") or from Appendix A ("Picture Books Everyone Should Know"). Show them the books that their children will be hearing in the children's session.

Libraries often have so many books that it can be overwhelming to parents. Showing books to them helps them to become familiar with authors and titles. If you have good books for them to choose from at the end of the session, they will be able to make good selections to take home to read to their children if the children have no choices of their own.

Talk about reading what children like, not necessarily what parents want to read or think is good for their children. It is important that children get to pick out books, so you should provide a variety of books for children to choose. Parents should allow children to pick out books, giving them time to find ones that they will enjoy. Often a child will pick a book that is too long or difficult for them to read or listen to. If a parent is not familiar with a book, they might want to read the book ahead of time. This will allow them to read those parts that are interesting and skip parts that will not affect the story when they read it later. Just as it is important for children to have balanced meals, it is important that they get a balance of reading materials.

Non-fiction is important as well a fiction. A suggested bibliography of non-fiction titles can be found in Appendix F. Books from popular television programs and movies are often the ones children recognize and what to read. Just as a parent would not feed their child only dessert and must introduce vegetables, fruits, and protein into a child's diet, they most also introduce good literature into a child's life. Good literature often has the more expansive vocabulary which is important for a child's mental growth.

Reading Aloud to Your Children

When reading a book, it is important that the parent talk about the cover. Can the child guess what the story might be about? Who wrote the book? What is the person who wrote the book called? What is an illustrator? Does the book have an illustrator? The parent can turn the book upside down or backward to see if the child will notice.

When reading aloud, parents are told to read in a dynamic voice. This makes it fun for the children. If a parent has difficult reading, they can talk about the pictures making the story the child's. If they are uncomfortable reading aloud, they can practice reading the book in private before reading it to the child. Remind the parents that it's okay to read out loud to yourself. You can suggest that they lock themselves in the bathroom or sit in the car and read the book out loud until they feel comfortable. The more you read out loud the better you will become.

One of the activities the children do in this first session is matching objects with the first letter of the object's name. Explain how the children have also been tracing or weaving letters to motivate them to identify letters. Show the parents how they can do this activity at home with magnetic letters and pictures from newspapers, magazines, or the Internet. The parents can also do this by pointing to an object, saying the name of the object and seeing if the child can give the letter that the object starts with.

The print motivation workshop is designed to prepare parents to see that their children enjoy books and reading. Remind parents that it is very important for them and their children to come to the next session when you will be covering print aware-ness. They should also return with their folders so they can keep their notes, and that they should bring back the empty folder after removing any work their children have completed during their session.

It is now time for them to return to the room where they registered to join their children for a story. If they are to take materials home, distribute the baggies now. They will also need to sign their children out of the session.

4

Print Motivation: First Session Children's Workshop

This session is about print motivation, which simply refers to the process of getting children excited about books and learning about books. You will be introducing the children to books and the alphabet, as well as learning how to listen and cooperate with others. For some children, this might be one of the first experiences in a group situation.

During each of the workshops, there will be an ABC song and at least one alphabet activity. You can add other alphabet songs and dances when it fits the day. Although full information about the opening of each workshop can be found in chapter 2, some of the information may be repeated here.

You will be introducing the letters of the alphabet so you will need pictures of objects for each letter of the alphabet. These may be cut from a worn-out alphabet book that you are ready to discard or you can find pictures in newspapers or magazines. You will need scissors, paper, and glue so you can cut them out, and paste onto a sheet or paper.

You should pre-cut letters, approximately six inches in size. You should make sure to make multiple copies of the more popular letters in case several children might want the same letter. If you are going to have children trace the letters, weave the letters, or make clay letters, you will also need the supplies necessary for those activities.

At the beginning of the session, sing a welcoming song (Appendix B). Then introduce a book from the "Print Motivation Bibliography" (Appendix E). Finish this segment by singing the ABC song (Appendix H).

Once the children have sung the ABC song, put up the alphabet on a flannel or magnetic board or write it on a white board. As you put up the letters ask the children to say the name of the letter after you. Give each child a picture of an object and ask each one to come up and tell the group what their object is and put it under or next to the letter that the object starts with. Sometimes a child might not know the object or may be shy about sharing, and you or the staff member will have to prompt them. This is a good opportunity to say the initial sounds of the words the children have chosen.

For example: if the object is a snake and the child has said snake; but doesn't know the letter the staff person might say what letter makes an *s* sound. If the child still doesn't respond, give him the answer by saying, "Snake starts with *s* which sounds like 'ssssss, snake.'"

Depending on the size of the group and their attention span, you might not want to give every child an object for this first part of the session. If the group is larger, you may want to have just three or four of the children come up the board. but make sure to let the children know that they will get a turn later.

When the children begin to lose interest, take a break from the alphabet and do an activity that lets the children move around. Some good activities include the Alphabet Dance, or the "Shake my Sillies or Head" and "Heads, Shoulder, Knee and Toes" rhymes. After allowing the children to move around, have them sit down and ask them to put on listening ears again. Read an alphabet book, for example *Chicka Chicka Boom Boom* by Bill Martin, or an alphabet book of your choice. Remember to coordinate the finger plays and books to be used in all the workshops.

Before reading the next book, talk about the book. You can show them the title, author, and illustrator. Don't be afraid to use a long word like *illustrator.* Words like these help to build a child's vocabulary. Hold the book upside down and ask the group if this is how we open a book. Begin reading the story from the back to see if anyone notices. Tell them about opening a book from right to left, and starting at the top and reading to the bottom. Point to the bottom and ask if that is the top. This will reinforce the concepts of top and bottom. Then tell them that we read left to right. Ask them to hold up their left hand. These concepts are important in learning how to read. After reading one or two books (see Appendix A for suggestions) and doing the finger play "Right hand, left hand" (Appendix B), sing one or two more songs. Active songs are good for this part of the session as the group will have been sitting for a while. After the children have one or more finger plays have them sit and look at books for a little while. This will give them practice in handling books.

Now is a good time to introduce another finger play or song from Appendix D, "Print Awareness and Print Motivation." Be sure to have some movement activities, as the children may be restless at this time.

Have some letter knowledge activities set up for the children to work at. Some of the activities can be:

- Tracing the letters of the alphabet.
- Weaving the letters of the alphabet.
- Using clay to make letters of the alphabet.
- Making a collage of objects for each letter of the alphabet from your pre-cut letters.

Children will need magazines or ads from newspapers and scissors to cut out pictures that start with the letter they have chosen. They will also need paper and glue. Once the children have chosen their letter and gotten their supplies, they can begin to look through the magazines for words or pictures representing words that begin with their letter. After gathering all the materials the children can begin gluing the pictures onto the large letter.

Since this workshop is on print motivation, you will want to give the children plenty of time to interact with books. Volunteers and staff can sit with small groups of children and look at a book. Or, if the children prefer, they can look at a book by themselves.

Parents will be joining the children at the end of the workshop for a story and the closing song. This is an opportunity for parents and children to share songs, finger-plays, and a book. Remind parents to sign their child out, leave their name tags, and come back for the next session, bringing their folders with them.

5

Print Awareness: Second Session Adult Workshop

In this chapter, we will be looking at print awareness, or in other words, being aware that print, letters, and words can be found everywhere and in many different forms and fonts. Parents will learn how to help their children recognize letters and words in places other than a book, and that we use these words in many ways.

Think about this statement, "It takes only 26 letters to make millions of words." This is the opening sentence in the book, *Words Are Not for Hurting,* by Elizabeth Verdick.[1]

For this second workshop, you will start with introductions and remind the parents of the purpose of the workshop. If participants have forgotten to bring paper, a pen, or their folder with them, you will need to provide them paper and a pen to take this week's notes. Remind them to bring the folder with them each week. Explain that you will be following the previous week's plan by introducing songs and finger plays that their children are also learning in their workshop, and ask the parents to participate with you so that they can repeat them with their children each week. Then ask them to sing the welcoming song and the ABC song. Sing them through once and then ask them to join in.

In this session, you will talk a little about brain development in children.[2] Babies are born with only one-fourth of their brains developed. The remaining three-fourths are developed after birth. By age three the brain has grown to about 80 percent of adult size and about 90 percent by age five. Research shows that what children experience in their first three years has a great deal to do with how well they can learn later. Parents can help with their child's brain development by your helping them acquire language skills. Children who have been talked to and read to by their parents have far more language skills than children who have not been talked to or read to by parents.

For many parents English may not be their first language. It is important that they understand that they should use the language they use most comfortably. Encourage them talk to and read to their children in the language they know best. Children have the ability to learn language very quickly at this age, and they will learn English quickly once they go to school.

After talking about brain development, take a break and do something fun. Have the parents stand and sing the ABC song, along with a couple of other songs or finger plays from Appendix B. Do the activity first and then have them do it with you. This is also a good time to talk about one or two books from the "Picture Books Everyone Show Know" bibliography in Appendix A.

When parents sit down again, begin by asking them the question, "Where do you find print?" Print is everywhere: labels, signs, cereal boxes, logos, magazines, to do list, on computers, and in recipes. Encourage parents to point out the different types of print, and explain how there are many ways that children can be introduced to print.

Moms and sometimes dads spend a great amount of time in the kitchen cooking. Children can participate and use pre-reading skills in many ways in the kitchen. As a recipe is being prepared, the child can be asked to bring different ingredients. A parent might want to set all the ingredients on a table so that the child can reach them. When an ingredient is needed, the child can be asked to bring it over to the parent who is cooking. The parent is there to give the child a clue. If the item name begins with the letter c and a c is on a yellow box, the parent can ask the child to bring a box with a name that starts with the letter c. If there are two words one starting, one with the letter c and the other starting with the letter t, explain that they can look for a yellow box with a c and a t. These kinds of clues reinforce other pre-reading skills such as colors and shapes.

When it is time to go to the grocery store, parent and child can make the shopping list together. Suggest that the parents gather grocery ads from the newspaper, a blank piece of paper, and some glue. The parents can tell the child what they are going to need at the store. The children can pick out the pictures of the items that the parents will be looking for in the store. Remind the parents that it is a good idea to help the child both cut out the picture and glue it onto the paper. The parent can print the name of the item next to the picture. Printing the name of the item reinforces that the picture represents a printed word.

At the grocery store, the parent can give the list and a pencil to the child and let them tell they what they need to find. When they get to the correct aisle, the parent can see if the child can find the product. Once the item has been found, this item can be checked or crossed off the list.

The grocery store is a great learning environment for children. They can start to recognize the different labels of their favorite foods. Grocery stores are also a place where you can talk about colors and shapes.

Children can help to organize the cupboards by helping put the groceries away, arranging all the products by type: cereal, vegetables, and soups. Then, these can be arranged alphabetically. This is an excellent way to get spices in alphabetical order.

When you are finished with talking about the grocery store, take a break and ask the parents of other ways that they can think of to point out words and letters to their children. Tell the story of someone who was told not to read at the dining table; but when there were products on the table like milk and cereal, these containers could be read. Even if this is not something you which happened to you, it doesn't matter. You can use it or make up a story of your own.

Introduce some of the books from the "Picture Books Everyone Should Know" bibliography (Appendix A) and introduce some finger plays and songs. After stretching and singing, go back to ways that children can be introduced to print in the world around them.

Remind the parents that play is important for a child's learning. Children should have a writing center, paper, scissors, markers, crayons, glue and other materials that they can use to practice their writing and use their creativity. Encourage parents to let children use magazines after they have been read and no longer needed to play with. The children can cut out pictures and paste words that describe the picture on a piece of paper. They can also practice writing the words.

Children should have easy access to paper, pencils, and crayons. Writing and drawing is important for hand and eye coordination and reinforces fine motor skills. Good eye-hand coordination is an important element in math. This is a good time to introduce parents to some of the books from the "Print Motivation Bibliography" (Appendix E).

When traveling in the car or bus, direct a child's attention to the signs and letters reading them aloud. An activity that can be done around the neighborhood is to take a simple camera and walk through the neighborhood letting the child take pictures of words that they recognize. You could do the same thing in a shopping area or mall. When looking at the developed pictures, have the child talk about the pictures, the words they see, and the beginning letters of words. They can then put the words in the pictures in alphabetical order. They can find pictures that have letters in their name. They can count the number of letters in each sign. The parent can write down the word and the number of letters. The child can then find the one that has the least number of letters and the one that has the most letters.

Another place that children can become aware of print is when eating out. Fast food restaurants often have pictures beside each item where orders are placed. Children can begin by looking at the picture and associating it with the item that they want. When using a menu at the table, the parent can point to words as they read the items on the menu. Many menus will also have pictures along with the item.

At the end of the session, remind parents that it is very important for them and their children to come to the next session when you will be covering letter knowledge. Ask them to make quick notes during the week of ways that they and their children became aware of print around them. Remind them also to bring their folder with them.

The parents will then rejoin their children for a story or song. They will also sign their children out of the session.

Notes

1. Elizabeth Verdick, *Words Are Not for Hurting* (Minneapolis, MN: Free Spirit Publishing, 2004), pg #.

2. The information given here is from two sources: Renea Arnold and Hell Colburn, "Oh! What a Smart Baby," *School Library Journal* 51 (Fall 2005): 37; and Kathy Hirsh-Pasek and Roberta Michnick, *Einstein Never Used Flash Cards: How Our Children REALLY Learn—and Why They Need to Play More and Memorize Less,* (Location: Rodale, 2003).

6

Print Awareness: Second Session Children's Workshop

The print awareness workshop is designed to help children become aware of the printed word beyond what they will see in a book. In this workshop, they will learn to look at print all around them.

Chapter 2, "Introduction to the Workshops," explains the preparation and opening for each workshop. Parents sign in their children, put on name tags, and leave for their session.

As with the first session, gather the children into a large circle on the floor asking them to leave all toys and books in the baskets. Once everyone has been seated, ask them to put on their listening ears. Next, reintroduce the staff and all volunteers. Remind the children of the rules: everyone sits puts on their listening ears, and takes turns talking. If they need to go to the bathroom, they should ask an adult to take them to their parents.

As you did during the previous workshop, start by saying "Good morning my name is (what you would like to be called). Next to me is (ask the child for a name)." The child next to you says their name, and everyone says good morning (name), continue around the room until everyone has said their name.

Sing a welcoming song and introduce a book from the "Print Motivation Bibliography" (Appendix E) or an alphabet book. You may find it difficult to find books that emphasizes print awareness. So substituting an alphabet book or a book from the "Picture Books Everyone Should Know" bibliography (Appendix A) is appropriate. Finish this segment by singing the ABC song (Appendix H).

Once you have sung the ABC song, you can begin an alphabet and object activity, in which the children work on connecting objects with their corresponding words. To start this activity, put the alphabet on a flannel or magnetic board, or write it out on a white board. As you place each letter on the board ask the children to repeat the name of the letter after you say it. Give a couple of the children a paper with one word on it, ask them to bring the word up and put it under or beside the letter that the word begins with. Again, you may have to assist the child with the letter. Some of the children may not be able to tell you what the word is. Assist as necessary.

Now is the time to do one or two activities such as singing another ABC song, or having them do the ABC Dance (see Appendix B). After this, if they are standing, ask them to sit down. Ask everyone to put on their listening ears on and read an alphabet book. You can then go back to the alphabet and object activity until everyone has had an opportunity to participate.

Give the children the opportunity to play with letters. Give them coloring sheets of letters, lace-up letters, and magnetic letters. The letter playtime can last between ten and fifteen minutes. When they have completed what they were working on, have them gather in a circle.

Show the children pictures of signs around the community such as signs for a bakery, barber shop, or coffee shop that they might recognize. Hold up one picture at a time and see if anyone can tell you what the sign says. You can also introduce road signs, (e.g., stop, one-way, no parking). Use other similar road signs that don't have words (e.g., curves, deer crossing, and railroad crossing) that children might recognize.

At this time read another book and do some finger plays from Appendix B. Be sure to include some movement activities too.

While they are waiting for their parents to return, it is time for the children to have some free playtime. Have some more letters and numbers activities for them to do. Other activities they can do are to take the pictures of signs and find signs that start with the letter of their first name, or they can sort them by the first letter of the sign. For example have them put all the signs that begin with the letter *b* together. Some children may want to choose a book to take home.

Parents will join their children for a closing activity, a song, or story. After this, remind parents to sign their children out, leave their name tags, and come back next week bringing their folders with them.

7

Letter Knowledge: Third Session Adult Workshop

The phrase letter knowledge refers to the knowledge that words are made up of individual letters. It also refers to the knowledge that each letter has its own name and that this name may be related to the sounds the letter makes when spoken. In the third session of the workshop, the children learn that letters are different from each other; and that the same letter may not look the same if it is written differently. Knowing all twenty-six letters will help children to know millions of words.

As with the other sessions, start with introductions. Have the parents to state his or her name and to tell at least one activity and book that they shared with their children during the week. Ask if they have any questions or comments about what took place during the week. Then sing the welcoming song.

Introduce the subject of the session, letter knowledge, and talk about what letter knowledge is. Explain to the parents how in order to read, children must understand that words are made up of individual letters and that each letter has its own name and sound. Having letter knowledge will help the child be able to sound out words.

Sing the ABC song. You can also introduce other alphabet songs (Appendix H).

Parents can begin teaching their children letter knowledge, by helping their children remember the names and shapes of the letters. Magnetic letters can be a very important tool. These are available in many stores and are inexpensive. If they want, they can make their own letters by using letters from the computer, putting them on heavy paper, covering with contact paper, and putting magnets on the back. Strips of magnets can be found at most craft stores. The computer can also be used to make the same letter in different fonts and sizes so that the child can see that the one letter can look different and still be the same. Also, parents can introduce upper and lower case letters.

The refrigerator door is one of the most useful teaching tools. Many parents, especially mothers, spend a great deal of time in the kitchen, and children like to be where their parents are. They can learn while the adults are working. As mentioned in chapter 5, there are many learning activities that children can do while mom or dad are cooking.

Children need to be able to recognize shapes and colors before they can start learning letters. Letters are made up of three shapes: straight, curved, and a combination of straight and curved. Parents can have their child line up all the straight-lined letters in a row. Then they can have them find all of the curved letters and finally all of the combination letters.

Experts in early childhood education recommend that children learn letters in a certain order. The first letter most children learn is the first letter of their first name and then the rest of the letters in their first name. Their last name will come much later.

Two good songs for letter knowledge are "BINGO" (Appendix H) and "My Bonnie Lies over the Ocean" (Appendix B). Ask parents to stand and sing these two songs. At this time share two books from the "Picture Books Everyone Should Know" bibliography (Appendix A).

Developing fine motor skills are those that occur in coordination with the eyes. These skills are essential in being able to write. Eye-hand coordination is also important in learning to read and to do math.

Children can work on their fine motor skills in many fun ways. One is tracing letters with one color of marker or crayon, and then tracing it again with another, and another. Use shaving cream, sand, oatmeal, or other tactile material that children can use to trace letters. Playing with various textures gives the child kinesthetic feedback.

Another activity that the parent and child can do together is to make letter cards. Using index cards, print an upper and lower case letter on each, and, on the back, paste a picture of an object and the word which begins with that letter. Use care to make sure that the object has a single letter. For example, the word *ball* begins with a *b*, whereas the words *race car* or a *school bus* have two sounds because they are two words.

Introduce two more books from the bibliographies, and then ask for questions or comments. Encourage parents to read and sing with their children and to look for ways in the coming week to play with letters. Parents then join their children for the closing session.

8

Letter Knowledge: Third Session Children's Workshop

The letter knowledge children's workshop begins like the previous workshops. Parents will sign in, spend a few minutes with their children looking at books, if they wish, and then go to their workshop.

All of the activities in this workshop will be around the alphabet and letters. Many activities, books, and finger plays are available to be used.

Start with introductions and sing the welcoming song. Introduce an alphabet book and finish this segment by singing the ABC song.

For an alphabet letter activity, hand out a letter card or picture card to each child. The card could have both the letter and a picture. Write a letter on the board, or put the letter on the flannel or magnetic board. The child whose picture begins with the letter or who has a matching letter card stands up. That child says the letter and the word of the picture (if they have picture cards). You should reinforce the answer and have all the children repeat the sound.

Do an activity at this time such as singing another alphabet song or have them do the ABC Dance (Appendix B). You could also play the game, "I Spy." Having children try to identify what you spy that begins with a certain letter. You can give added hints if needed. For example, "I spy something that begins with *b*. You can read it." (*book*) Have the child who correctly identifies the object go to the board and write the letter. Have everyone practice saying the word with emphasis on the first letter.

To reinforce the shapes of the letters draw a straight line on a white board and ask the children what you have drawn. Explain that many letters are made up of straight lines. Put up the letters made up of straight lines. Have the children call out the name of the letter as you put it up. After they have identified straight-lined letters, draw a half circle to demonstrate a curved line. Ask them to identify the shape. This might be more difficult and you might have to help them.

Next ask them to identify letters with curved lines. The third type of letters are those with both a curved line and a straight line. To demonstrate these kinds of letters, draw a curved line over a straight line. Have the children identify combination letters. After demonstrating the difference between straight, curved, and combination letters, give the children a chance to identify letters by the type of lines they are made up of. Randomly write a letter on the board or put up a letter, and ask the children to identify the letter and the type of line.

Give the children a red, green and blue crayon, if you don't have enough for each child, have them form groups to share crayons. Give them a worksheet that has the alphabet. These can be found in books or on the Internet. Ask them to trace the straight-lined letters with the red crayon, and the curved letters with the green crayon, and lastly the combination letters with the blue crayon.

It is now time for some movement. Have a volunteer place large-form letters or large cut-out letters while the children are working on their worksheet (use painter's tape to create letters on the floor about three feet apart). Gather the children in a circle and explain what they will be doing and that it is important to keep their listening ears on so they can hear the directions. Ask them to tiptoe to a straight-lined letter (more than one child can be on a letter). When everyone is on a letter, ask them to crawl to a curved letter. They can then hop to a combined curved- and straight-lined letter. Continue with different ways of moving to different letters. The number of letters you have them move to will depend on your time and the enthusiasm of the children. When it is time to change activities have the children freeze in place. Then ask them to walk back to the circle area. Instead of having them move to a straight, curved, or combination letter you can also have them move to a different letter.

Another more active movement is to have children perform an action that represents a letter. If you say *h*, they hop. If you say *w*, they walk. If you say *j*, they jump. If you say *y*, they yawn. You can give them a prop such as a ball and have them do things with it depending on the letter called out. For example, say *b*, and they bounce the ball. Say *t*, and they toss the ball. Say *c*, and they catch the ball. They do not need a ball, they can pretend to have one.

If you want an activity that is a quiet sitting activity, give the children a clipping, from a newspaper or magazine, and have them circle or highlight all the examples they can find of a specified letter. You can challenge them to find a certain number of occurrences, such as seven. The number should vary with how common the letter is.

Back in the circle area, read a book, say a nursery rhyme, sing "BINGO" (Appendix H) and "My Bonnie Lies over the Ocean" (Appendix B) or another song from Appendix H ("Letter Sounds for Letter Day Activities"). After singing a couple songs, end with the good-bye song. While they are waiting for their parents they can chose a book, work with the lacing letters, or color a worksheet.

When the parents have joined their children read a story from the "Letter Knowledge, Letter Awareness" bibliography or sing the closing song. Remind the parents to sign their children out and to bring their folders with them the following week.

9

Vocabulary: Fourth Session Adult Workshop

The fourth session of the workshop focuses on helping children learn vocabulary, by helping them to begin to recognize written words and to understand that each word has its own particular meaning. Knowing the meaning of individual words or being able to figure out the meaning is essential to being able to comprehend what is read. Children must learn to recognize printed words and know what they mean so they will have a larger vocabulary. Research has shown that children who have a larger vocabulary are more likely to become better readers and are more successful in school. One way of increasing a child's vocabulary is to talk to them. In this session, you can suggest that parents should encourage family discussions. This means turning off the television while having an evening meal. You can also suggest to the parents that it is a good idea to set up some ground rules first. These rules could include making sure that everyone should be allowed to talk, and that everyone needs to take turns to talk. The conversation should be pleasant, fun, and a time for everyone to be listening to what is said.

After introducing the session's topic, you can share some examples of good vocabulary building books from the "Vocabulary Bibliography" (Appendix I) and the "Picture Books Everyone Should Know" bibliography (Appendix A). This is also a good time to do some finger plays from "Finger Plays and Songs" (Appendix B) and to sing two or three songs. You should make sure to have the adults sing the same songs that are being taught to their children.

After singing songs, you can talk with the parents about different ways they can help their children engage with new vocabulary words. For example, when the child talks with a parent, the parent can add more detail to what they say. For example, if the child says, "I saw a truck," the parent can respond by asking open-ended questions, "What color was they truck?" By encouraging children to add descriptive phrases to their sentences, parents can help children use a wide range of vocabulary. You can also suggest when talking to their children, parents shouldn't be afraid to add descriptive words or to use so-called big words, or in other words, words that might not usually be used when talking to children.

If for non-native English speaking parents, encourage them to speak in the language that is most comfortable to them. What is most important is that children hear language, and parents don't need not worry if they prefer another language. Children will quickly learn to respond in both languages. The preschool years are an excellent time for children to learn languages. Their brain is developing in a way that makes language connection easy.

Another suggestion you can give the parents is that when reading a book to their child, they can talk about the story and the pictures as they read together. When the parent reads a word that is unfamiliar to the child, it is a nice opportunity to stop and talk about the word. See if the child can guess what it means from the picture and from the story. If the parent is unfamiliar with the word, they can get a dictionary, especially a children's dictionary, and look it up. Remind the parents that a children's dictionary is an important book for every child to have. Many children love to read dictionaries to find funny or unusual words. Using a dictionary helps a child learn that there is a place to go when they need to know what a word means or how to correctly spell a word.

A dictionary doesn't have to be used only when you need to look up the meaning of a word. You can also use a dictionary just to look at, especially picture dictionaries. Suggest to the parents that they can look at dictionaries with their children. The child can point to pictures and to the corresponding words. The child can also say the word aloud, and then going one step further, the parent and child can make up a short, two or three sentence story about the word. Show the parents examples of good children's dictionaries and give them a list with costs (Appendix K).

You can also remind the parents that when reading to their child, they can read non-fiction books as well as fiction books. Fathers and boys especially like to read non-fiction. If a parent is planning a trip the parent can read to the child about where they are going or what they might be seeing. Children are fascinated by the world around them. Pets, trucks, and airplanes are good examples of different kinds of objects that fascinates them. They are also interested in things they see on television or in the movies. Good examples of things in movies that children love are dinosaurs, volcanoes, and monsters. You may not want to read every word; but the pictures help to give information too. Show examples of non-fiction books from the "Non-Fiction (Informational) Bibliography" (Appendix F).

To help children learn that objects around the house have names, which are words and what those words look like, parents can put labels on items. Parents may want to start in the child's bedroom and label one or two objects each day. Once a child has begun to associate an object with the word, parents can try switching them around and see if they can find the ones that are mixed up. Parents can put a label on an object in another room and see if the child can find it. Suggest to the parents to make it a game. It doesn't have to be done every day or for a long period of time. Remind the parents that it is always best to keep their learning activities fun and fresh. When children do a good job, it is important to compliment them. In the same respect if the child makes a mistake, it is important to not criticize them. Instead, it is best to give them encouragement and then help them find the right answer.

Children often have favorite words that they say. Parents can create a word box in which children can keep these words. You can provide parents with the following instructions for making a word box:

> Take a simple box such as a shoebox. Cover it with paper, an old grocery bag, wrapping paper or newspaper. Anything will do. Let your child help you and then let them decorate it. Using scissors, drawing and writing helps develop fine motor skills that are important for developing reading skills. Once you have your box and small pieces of paper or old business cards, which work well for this activity, to write the word of the day on, let your child pick the word of the day. Spell the word as you write it. This reinforces that letters make words. The next day, have the child choose a new word. Write it on a paper or card and then you and the child read it together. Each day a new word is added. When you put in a new word take out one or more of the old words and have the child read the word. When the box has many cards in it, you may want to remove some of the words already in the box. The child can add more than one word each day. During the day, they can sit with their box and look through it saying the words as they pull them out. If they, want they can discard words that they do not like. There is no single right way to use the word box; it is up to the child. When it is no longer interesting; put the box aside. The child will want to look at it again at another time.

After giving parents instructions for the word box, you can remind them that a good way to help their child with vocabulary is to have their child help with grocery shopping. Parents can start the morning with making up the grocery list. It's good to include the child in the whole grocery shopping process. As parents walk, ride, or drive to the store, they can point out letters and words on signs as they see them. Parents can talk about the colors of the fruits and vegetable with their child, and ask them to tell what colors are which. On the way home, parents can have their child recount the order in which the items were placed in the grocery cart.

At the end of the session, the parents rejoin the children. Remind the parents to bring their folders the next week.

10

Vocabulary: Fourth Session Children's Workshop

All of the activities in this workshop are meant to help children develop vocabulary, by having children use adjectives to describe objects and by helping them understand that there are many ways to describe something.

Gather the children into a large circle on the floor. Ask them to leave all toys and books in the baskets. Once everyone has been seated, ask them to put on their listening ears. Again, introduce the staff and volunteers. Remind them of the rules. Start again with getting to know each other, and continue around the room until everyone has said their name.

Sing the welcoming song you have chosen. Then introduce a book from the "Vocabulary Bibliography" (Appendix I). A good book for this workshop is Audrey Wood's *The Napping House.* Read the book, and then finish this segment by singing the ABC song. Finish this segment by singing "Down by the Bay" by Raffi. This song has many descriptive and rhyming words. After the song, you can also do a finger play, such as "The Itsy Bitsy Spider" (Appendix H).

To teach children that objects have names and that the names are made up words, go around the room and put labels on objects. Make the labels large enough for the children to see from where they are sitting or standing. Do not label every object, as this will overwhelm the children. Go around the room and point to each of the labels, read it and then point to each letter spelling out the word. Tell the children that when they see these letters in this order, the letters make up the word that is the name for the object. Have the children go back to the circle. Give children labels for objects that are in the room and then ask the children to put the correct label on the corresponding object. Because they may not be able to remember what the letters spelled, there may be more than one label on an object. When all of the labels have been replaced, go around the room and look at each label. If the label is not correct, say the word pointing out each letter. Then have a child put the label on the correct object.

The last exercise is to try to get the children describe the object to the group. Do not force them if they do not want to participate. When a child is describing the object, you can help them by asking open-ended questions. For example, if the object is a table, have them describe the color. If the child says that the table is brown, you can ask them, "Is it light or dark brown?" You could also ask them other questions about the table, such as, "What are the legs of the table like? Are they skinny or fat? Are they made of wood or metal?"

The children have been doing a lot of thinking, which is hard work, so now is the time for some movement. Start out with the ABC Dance (Appendix B). While they are in a circle do "The Hokey Pokey" and then "Ring Around the Rosy." Now that they are all standing, you can also have them do "Teddy Bear, Teddy Bear" and have them all sit down (Appendix B). Read the story *Ella Sarah Gets Dressed* by Margaret Irvine. This is an excellent book for vocabulary because of the description of each piece of clothing that Ella is putting on. When her young friends arrive at the door, stop and discuss what each of the children are wearing. Then ask the children to describe something that they are wearing. You may have to encourage them to go into more detail. If they say a shirt, ask them if it is a t-shirt or a shirt with buttons, does it have a picture on it, is the picture big or small, is there another name for big? Be sure to finish the story.

After the story, ask the children if they learned a new word during the morning and if they can remember it or if they have a favorite word. Tell them that they are going to make a word box, and they can put a word on a piece of paper or card. Old business cards are excellent for this activity. After the child writes a word on the card, they put the card into the box. They will take their boxes home with them at the end of the day. The next day or later in the day they can open their box and read the words in the box. But first they must decorate their box.

At the tables there should be a box for each child that has been wrapped with paper and materials for them to use in decorating their box. These materials can include anything from stickers, stamps and stamp pads, and crayons, to magic markers, scissors, paper, and glue. Let the fun begin! When they have finished decorating their box, help them write their name on the box and to write the word of the day on a card to put in the box. When they are finished they may play with the toys, the magnetic letters, or look at books until their parents return.

When the parents come, read a story to close the session. Remind the parents to sign out their children and a select a book, and also to remember to bring their folders for the next session.

11

Narrative Skills: Fifth Session Adult Workshop

For the purposes of this workshop, narrative skills are defined as being able to tell a story. Children who have narrative skills know that stories have a beginning, middle and end. In this session you will be introducing the subject of narrative skills, and explaining ways parents can help their child gain these skills through wordless picture books, storytelling, writing letters, and retelling stories.

Start this session with introductions asking everyone to give their name and to tell the group at least one activity or book that they shared with their children during the week. Ask if they have any questions or comments about what took place during the week. Then sing the welcoming and ABC songs.

Introduce the subject of the session, narrative skills. Explain that narrative skills include knowing how to tell a story or describe an event, and knowing that a story has a beginning, middle, and end. Narrative skills help young children organize the world around them. Share a book from the "Narrative Bibliography" (Appendix L). Then sing a song that has a story line to it. An example is the "Farmer's in the Dell" (Appendix B), which starts with the farmer and ends with the cheese standing alone.

Narrative skills can also include dialogic readings, or in other words hear-and-say readings. In this kind of storytelling, the child can become the storyteller and the adult can be the questioner, listener, and audience. Adults ask open answer questions about the story. The idea of asking questions and having children answer can also be done when watching television, videos, and with everyday experiences. The purpose is to get the child to respond by telling something about the television show, the video, or even what they did playing with a friend.

Storytelling is a great way to introduce narrative. Family stories are a fun way for children to learn about their family and to introduce them to the idea of narration. Family stories have a beginning, a middle, and end. In the evening around the dinner table, everyone can tell something about their day. Parents can help their children tell the story in chronological order.

Demonstrate storytelling by telling a story for the parents. Emphasize that storytelling doesn't have to be eloquent or elaborate.

You can also introduce parents to wordless books, for example, April Wilson's *Magpie Magic: A Tale of Colorful Mischief*. To demonstrate how to use a wordless book to practice telling stories, take a book apart and then number the pages in case they get out of order. Pass the pages or pictures around the group. If there are more pages or pictures than participants, pass them around again. Have the parent hold up their picture and tell what is happening as if it were a part of the story. When they get their page or picture say, "What will happen next?" or "What is happening now?" Explain that this is how they can use a wordless book with their child.

Share books from the "Narrative Bibliography" (Appendix L) or from the "Picture Books Everyone Should Know" bibliography (Appendix A). Because most libraries have so many books, picking books out at the library can be overwhelming to many parents. When you bring books with you for them to choose, it gives parents more confidence in selecting books. It is important to share as many books with them as possible.

Another activity that strengthens a child's ability to sequence events is to have children write a letter to a relative or friend telling about something that happened to them that day. Parents can help their child write a letter that has a beginning, middle and end. For instance, I received a letter from a niece that said, "I have two new hamsters (beginning), their names are Peter and Tom (middle), and they live in a cage (ending)." Since most children won't be able to actually write a letter that the recipient can read, let them write the letter in their pretend writing and then the parents can have the child tell them what they wrote and the parent can add it to the bottom of the child's letter. This way, the recipient will be able to read the letter. The letter can be e-mailed but some grandparents still enjoy receiving letters in the mail and children have always enjoyed receiving mail. Encourage the recipient of the letter to write back to the child so they can have the fun of getting mail.

Read a story that develops narrative skills. Two good choices are *The Mitten* by Jan Brett or *Too Much Noise* by Ann McGovern. Stop during the reading and ask the parents what they think will happen next or stop before the end and ask how they think the story will end. Explain to parents that this is what they can do with their child. Emphasize that they don't have to do this with every book.

Other good stories for reinforcing narrative skills are traditional folk tales such as, "Goldilocks and The Three Bears" and "The Three Little Pigs." After reading the story parents can ask their children what happened at the very beginning of the story. Then, they can ask what came next and finally what happened at the end of the story.

A last activity could be "Guess the Ending." Three books that work well with this are *Alexander and the Terrible, Horrible, No Good, Very Bad Day* by Judith Viorst, *The Mitten* by Jan Brett, and Mercer Mayer's *There's a Nightmare in My Closet*. Parents can read a part of the book with their child and have them guess the ending. The important thing is to accept whatever ending the child provides, even if it doesn't make sense to the parent. Then finish the book. The parent may then talk with their child about how the author's ending compares with what their child guessed.

You may wish to have books from these bibliographies or others you may choose from the shelf for parents to select one to take home. When the session concludes, the parents will return to collect their children and to listen to another story or the closing song.

12

Narrative Skills: Fifth Session Children's Workshop

All of the activities in this workshop will be around developing children's narrative skills, such as sequencing and using specific details.

Begin the workshop by gathering the children into a large circle on the floor. Ask them to leave all toys and books in the baskets. Once everyone has been seated, ask them to put on their listening ears. Again, introduce the staff and volunteers. Remind them of the few rules, and then have everyone go around the room saying their name.

Sing the welcoming song you have chosen. Remember that you will be using the same song every week, and the song you choose should be the same as used in the adult workshop. After singing the welcoming song, introduce a book from the "Picture Books Everyone Should Know" (Appendix A). A good book for this workshop is Eric Carle's *Very Hungry Caterpillar*. Finish this segment by singing the ABC song.

Once you have sung the ABC song, put up the alphabet on a flannel or magnetic board, or write it on a white board. As you put up the letters ask the children to say the name of the letter after you. For the next activity you will need some plastic food, a paper grocery bag, or a plastic shopping basket. Tell the children that they are going to the grocery store. Place the food in a large basket or sack, and then ask a child to pick out a food item, giving it to the instructor. Ask the children what the item is; what letter the item starts with; what color, shape, and texture the item is? Elicit answers from the entire group. The food then goes into the basket or bag. Once every child has a turn, start a story about going to the grocery story, and what we bought, pulling each item out of the bag. Once all the items are out have the children see if they can remember in which order they found the items. This is a good activity to teach sequencing.

Other activities that can be done with the food, include sorting items in different ways: alphabetically, by color, or by texture. The items can also be counted to see how many items were purchased.

Now is the time to introduce the nursery rhyme, "Hey, Diddle, Diddle." While reciting the rhyme, ask the group which animal went over the moon and what happened next, until the nursery rhyme has been completed. Repeat the rhyme one more time. Sing two or more songs, or do a couple finger plays from the list of finger plays that the parents have been given.

Read or tell a story. Good stories that illustrate narration include "The Little Old Woman Who Swallowed a Fly," "Bark, George," "Little Red Hen," and "Goldilocks and the Three Bears". All of these stories contain sequences that are repeated. While reading the story ask the children to guess what will happen next. Before reading the ending ask them to guess what they think will happened. Sharing a wordless book also does this well because you can get the children to tell the story for you. Ask open-ended questions and ask them for details about the illustrations.

It is now time to stand and do some stretching and movement activities such as "Shake the Sillies," "Head, Shoulder, Knees and Toes," or "The Hokey Pokey." The last two help children identify parts of the body and the concepts of in and out. The ABC Dance has good movement activities that emphasis the alphabet and the concept of right and left, forward and backward. Another alphabetic movement activity is to place large-form letters, cut-out letters, or letters created with painter's tape and put them around the room, about three feet apart. Ask the children to tiptoe to the *c*. When everyone is at *c* ask them to hop to the *y* and continue until they have reached all the letters. Then say "freeze," having them freeze in place. Once they are frozen ask them to move back to the circle.

Narration is the process of telling a story. This activity helps children learn how to begin a story and how to use specific details when telling a story. To start this activity, bring out a box of props, or a storytelling box. The props in the box can be anything: an unusual umbrella, a pair of funny glasses (such as one with a nose and bushy eye-brows), a beautiful scarf, a tiara, a whistle or other musical instrument, or a beautiful toy horse, From this box choose three items. Start by telling the children that the story will need a problem and a setting. Tell them the story can start with the phrase. "Once upon a time." Then have the children complete the phrase. Tell them that there are three parts of a story: a beginning, a middle or a "what happens next" part, and finally an ending.

Here is a story to get you started: "In a beautiful garden a little girl had a *gorgeous scarf*; but the wind blew it away. She ran after the scarf, not looking where she was going and ran right into a scary looking man, wearing funny-looking *glasses, with bushy eyebrows.* He said not to be afraid; he had a magic *whistle* that could find all lost things. All the girl had to do was to turn around three times and blow the whistle as loud as she could. The girl turned around three times, blew as hard and a loud as she could on the whistle and waited. Before long an elegant wonderful white *horse* came galloping through the mountains with the gorgeous scarf around its neck. The little girl returned the whistle to the scary man and rode the wonderful white horse back to her enchanted garden."

Read the book *Why Did the Chicken Cross the Road* by Jon Agee and other illustrators, which has wonderful illustrations. Pick your favorite picture and ask the children to tell you from the picture why the chicken crossed the road. You could also have them look at the book and choose a picture to explain. After they have looked at the book, as a group have them make up a story about why the chicken crossed the road. Write down what they tell you. Keep it short. Three to five sentences is enough. After they have told the story, read the story back to them. Ask if there is anything they want to change? When the story is finished, have the children go to tables that have been set up with white paper for illustrating their story. Also on the table are markers, crayons, scissors, paper, and glue. Now is the time for the children to illustrate their story. After the workshop is over, make copies of the story and staple them on to each child's illustration.

Color sheets of the nursery rhymes, lacing letters, letters, and numbers to trace and other activities are laid out on tables. Children can work on the activities of their choice.

About ten minutes prior to the end of the workshop, ask the group to put away their work sheets, their crayons, and other supplies, and have them gather in a circle. Back in the circle, say a nursery rhyme and sing "BINGO" or another song. While waiting for their parents, they can look at the books.

Once the parents have arrived, read another story or sing the closing song. Remind the parents to sign their children out, and to remember to return folders at the next session.

13

Phonological Awareness: Sixth Session Adult Workshop

Phonological awareness is the ability to distinguish parts of speech, such as syllables and phonemes. Children develop phonological awareness through verbal communication. A word can be broken down into syllables and phonemes. Phonemic awareness is being able to hear the smallest sounds in words, for example, being able to hear individual sounds. Phonological awareness also includes the ability to hear how phonemes work together to create syllables. It also includes the ability to pick out the sound a word starts with and the ability to recognize rhymes.

Begin the workshop with introductions. An easy exercise is to clap out the syllables in your name. Demonstrate this for the parents using your name. Then go around the room and ask parents to clap out the syllables of their name. Tell them to do this with their children until the children are comfortable with clapping out their names.

To make this more fun, say the rhythmic chant, "Bippity Bippity Bumblebee, Tell me what your name should be." Point to a parent and ask them to "whisper their name while clapping." Ask several parents to do this. Repeat the chant and ask several parents to silently enunciate each syllable as they clap.

Then sing the opening song. Review the five pre-reading skills that were covered in the previous sessions: print motivation, print awareness, letter knowledge, vocabulary, and narrative skills,. Ask the participants about activities that they did during the week. What were their successes? What challenges are they encountering? Take time to discuss each, especially the challenges seeing if the group can suggest solutions.

This is the last of the six pre-reading skill workshops. Phonological awareness is the ability to hear different sounds. Then introduce books from the "Phonological Awareness Bibliography" (Appendix M) and from the "Picture Books Everyone Should Know" bibliography (Appendix A).

Then introduce Dr. Seuss and easy readers. In the 1950s, readers for the early grades were boring and bland and no one wanted to read. Dr. Seuss knew he could do better. When he was commissioned to write an easy reader using the 200 new reader vocabulary, he wrote *The Cat in the Hat*. *The Cat in the Hat* is still popular today, and there is a new award named for Dr. Seuss for the best easy reader of the year. The first book to be awarded the Dr. Seuss award was *Henry and Mudge and the Great Grandpas* written by Cynthia Rylant and illustrated by Suçie Stevenson in 2006.

Read, Steve Webb's *Tanka, Tanka, Skunk*. This is a good example of a book that emphasizes rhyming words. Talk about one or two of other books from the "Phonological Awareness Bibliography" (Appendix M) and "Picture Books Everyone Should Know" bibliography (Appendix A).

Sing the song "This Old Man" and the finger play "Say and Touch," or sing one or two songs or finger plays of your choice that emphasize rhyming words.

The next activity is to introduce parents to challenging their children with synthesizing words from their separate phonemes. In this activity, you can show parents how to play with phonemes to made new words. Begin the exercise by introducing the word *ox*. Then ask the parents what would happen if a new sound was added to the beginning word *ox*? Say, "For example, the sound, *f, fox*. What other letters can we add to the word *ox* to make a new sound, such *b - ox*?" Tell the parents that they can do this activity with their children.

Then present two Easy Reader series that play with phonemes. Colin Hawkins has written a series, which is in many libraries, though it is out of print in the United States. Two titles include, *Jen the Hen* and *Pat the Cat*. Show examples of these books. The other series is "Easy Words to Read" by Phil Cox. Three titles are *Ted in a Red Bed, Goose on the Loose*, and *Fox on a Box*.

Here is another activity that parents can do with their children. Using magnetic letters on the refrigerator, parent can put up the several letter combinations such as *ox, ig,* and *at*. Then the parent can have their child add letters to make new words. Sometimes, the child will add a letter that makes a silly-sounding word, that's not a real word. If this happens, the parent can see if the child is able to tell the difference between a made-up word and a real word. Sometimes the child will put up a letter that makes the same sound; but is spelled differently (e.g., *s-o-x* instead of *socks*). In both the case of the made-up word or misspelled word, this activity is a great time for parents to explore with their children how to look up words in a children's dictionary.

After introducing this activity, have the parents do a movement exercise such as "Head, Shoulders, Knees and Toes," or sing the "Wheels on the Bus" or other finger plays and songs in Appendix B. Conclude with "Teddy Bear, Teddy Bear."

Introduce the book *A Hunting We Will Go* by John Langstaff using the flannel board. This is a good example of rhyming words. Go through the book once. The next time instead of saying the rhyming word, wait for the parent to respond with a word.

Another way of hearing the syllables is to say a word and clap out the syllables. Show the picture of a butterfly. Say the word slowly clapping each syllable, *but-ter-fly*. Then say it fast clapping to each phoneme: but (clap) ter (clap) fly (clap).

Also, look for other words within a word, such as *hotdog* and *airplane*. Show the parent a picture of an airplane. Say it slowly, *air—plane* and then fast *airplane*. Explain how parents can show a picture and then the written word to see if their child can identify the two words (e.g., *fire* and *truck*).

Another exercise parents can do with children is a listening activity. This activity helps children hear and say parts of a word. Tell the parents, "Make up a list of words: baseball, raincoat, sunshine, and motorcycle. This will help you to know which words to say when playing this game. Say one of the words you have chosen and then say the word again leaving off part of the word, that is, say *sunshine*. Now say the word again, this time leaving off the first part of the word, *sun*, and ask the child what was left off. As you do this, rotate from leaving off the first syllable and then the last. This is a fun game to play in the car."

Another fun activity that children enjoy is saying riddles. Here is a rhyming riddle that parents can use with their children:

I am thinking of something
that you wear on your feet.
Its name rhymes with rocks. (socks)

Or,

I am thinking of a something
that you wear on your head.
Its name rhymes with cat. (hat)

Here are a couple more rhyming riddles that parents can use. The parent should tell their child that the answer has two words that rhyme.

What is big and furry and purrs? (fat cat)
What kind of dance happens in autumn? (fall ball)
What is large and oinks? (big pig)

Remind the parents that if they want to learn other riddles, there many riddle books available.

Before returning to the children, remember to thank the parents for giving of their time to come and learn how they can get their child ready to read. Tell them that you have enjoying getting to know them. Ask them if there are any special ideas, books, or songs that they would like to share, or any experiences that they have had at home to share. Ask them also to fill out the evaluation. The evaluation is an important tool to assist you in learning what is working, what you need to adjust, and it may give you some good quotations that you can use in publicizing the program next time. Remind parents that there will be a celebration when they pick up their children. See chapter 14, "Phonological Awareness: Sixth Session Children's Workshop" to learn more about the plans for the celebration.

14

Phonological Awareness: Sixth Session Children's Workshop

Gather the children into a large circle on the floor. Ask them to leave all toys and books in the baskets. Once everyone has been seated, ask them to put on their listening ears. Next, reintroduce the staff and all volunteers. Remind the children of the few rules, and have the children go around the room until everyone has said their name. For this session, when the child says his name, you can repeat the name clapping the syllables of their names (e.g., *Ro* (clap) *bert* (clap), or *Ry* (clap) *an* (clap)). After the instructor has said and clapped the names, ask the children to repeat the exercise.

A variation of the introduction being shared with parents would be to start off with a rhythmic chant, "Bippity Bippity, Bumblebee, tell me what your name should be." Then point to one of the children, and they respond by giving their name enunciating and clapping to each syllable. Variations of the clapping would be to whisper the name clapping to each syllable or to have the children silently enunciate each syllable with clapping.

Next, sing the welcoming song you have chosen. Then introduce a book, *Tanka Tanka Skunk* by Steve Webb, or *Dunk Skunk* by Michael Rex or another from the "Phonological Awareness Bibliography" (Appendix M). Finish this segment by singing the ABC song.

The next activity will demonstrate synthesizing words from their separate phonemes. This is a fun activity to introduce a puppet and stuffed animals. Using a puppet or animal, say the word *monkey*. Then say each syllable slowly: *mon* and then *key*. Then say it fast, *monkey*. Continue with other words that have two syllables. Go back to words that you have already said.

Another activity with a puppet is to introduce the puppet to the children and tell them that one of them is going to help with the next activity. Tell them that you are going to whisper a word to the puppet. Whisper the word, *sunshine*. Then have the puppet whisper back to the child the word *shine*. Tell the children that this is not the word you whispered to him and ask what word goes with *shine*. They may come up with other words that have the word *shine* in them. This is fine, too, because there can be several words that end with *shine*. After you have tried a few words leaving off the first part of the word reverse the order and have the puppet say the first part of the word.

Sing two songs "This Old Man" and "Down by the Bay" by Raffi. Do the finger play, "Say and Touch" (Appendix B) and one or two other finger plays. This session on phonological awareness is in part about learning how to rhyme words; and a good book that demonstrates rhymes, which is also fun to do, is *Oh A-Hunting We Will Go* by John Langstaff. Tell this story using a flannel or magnetic board. Tell the story once without stopping. Then read the story a second time and as you put up the figure of the fox say, "Put him in a . . ." and pause and wait for the children to come up with a rhyming word for *fox*. In the beginning, you may have to prompt the children.

To help children develop their ability to hear differences between what they expect to hear and what they actually hear, have children close their eyes and listen. Recite or read aloud a familiar nursery rhyme. Every once in a while change the words or wording, change the sense to something that is nonsense, and challenge the children to raise their hand when they hear something that doesn't sound right. Examples of changes are:

"Sing a song of sixpence" to "Song of sixpence sing"
"Baa, baa, black sheep" to "Baa, baa, purple sheep"
"Humpty Dumpty sat on a wall" to "Humpty Dumpty wall on a sat"
"One, two buckle my shoe" to "One, two shuckle my boo"

It is now time to have some physical activity. Stand up and do some movement activities. Do the "Hokey Pokey" or the ABC Dance.

The next activity is a rhyming picture collage. Photocopy several copies of pictures of words that rhyme, for example, a baseball bat, a cat, a hat, and a rat, or a pig and a wig, or a hen and a pen. Put the pictures on a table, along with paper, crayons, and glue. Ask the children to select pairs of pictures that rhyme and have them glue them on the paper and color the pictures. You can also help the child print the names of the objects below the object.

About fifteen minutes before the closing, ask the children to put their names on their work sheets, pick up crayons and other materials, and gather back in the circle. Depending on the time, you can do another story, sing a song or finger play. Then sing the closing song. Children can look at books while waiting for their parents.

This is the final session of the program, and it is always fun to celebrate what everyone has been learning over the past four or six weeks or months. The celebration can take any form that fits into your budget and library. You should allow around twenty minutes, so that you have enough time for story time, and some of finger plays and songs that have been learned. Try reading some books from the bibliographies that haven't been used during the program. You might want to give parents an opportunity to speak, if they didn't do so in the adult workshop. Then call each parent and child to come forward and present them with a certificate (Appendix N). If the budget allows a book, the choice of title is your decision. For the parents, the new book by Rosemary Wells, *My Shining Star,* a collection of nursery rhymes, or a children's CD would be appropriate. I like to give the mothers a carnation. Then celebrate with food. Make the celebration yours. Close by singing the closing song the one that has been used at the end of each session, and a big thank you and encourage them to keep reading and using the library.

APPENDIXES

Appendix A

Picture Books Everyone Should Know

Aadema, Verna. *Why Mosquitoes Buzz in People's Ears: A West African Tale.* New York: Dial Press, 1975.
A tale about the disaster that befalls the jungle when a mosquito tells lies.

Ada, Alma Flora. *Gathering the Sun: An Alphabet in Spanish and English.* New York: Lothrop, Lee, and Shephard Books, 1997.

Alborough, Jez. *My Friend Bear.* Cambridge, Mass.: Candlewick Press, 1998.
Eddie and his teddy bear meet a very big bear in the woods. They become good friends.

Allard, Harry. *Miss Nelson is Missing.* Boston: Houghton Mifflin, 1977.
In Room 371, the student's good-natured teacher disappears and they get a vile substitute.

Asch, Frank. *Just Like Daddy.* Englewood Cliffs, N.J.: Prentice Hall, 1981.
A very young bear describes all his activities during the day that are just like his daddy's.

Aylesworth, Jim. *Old Black Fly.* New York: Holt, 1992.
A mischievous old black fly romps through the alphabet as he has a very busy, bad day.

Baker, Keith. *Big Fat Hen.* San Diego: Harcourt Brace, 1994.
Big Fat Hen counts to ten with her friends and all their chicks.

Bang, Molly. *Ten, Nine, Eight.* New York: Greenwillow Books, 1983.
Numbers from ten to one are part of this lullaby. The story takes place in a room with a little girl going to bed.

Barrett, Judi. *Cloudy with a Chance of Meatballs.* New York: Atheneum, 1978.
Chewandswallow is a town where it rains soup and juice, and snow is mashed potatoes.

Base, Graeme. *Water Hole.* New York: Harry N. Abrams, 2001.
An ever-growing number of animals visit a watering hole as the water dwindles.

Bemelmans, Ludwig. *Madeline.* New York: Viking Press, 1967.
The rhyming story of a schoolgirl, who lives in a house covered by vines in Paris.

Brett, Jan. *The Mitten.* New York: Putnam, 1989.
Several animals sleep snugly in Nicki's lost mitten until the last animal, sneezes.

Brown, Marcia. *Stone Soup.* New York: Scribner, 1947.
When three hungry soldiers make soup of water and stones, the town enjoys a feast.

Brown, Margaret. *Goodnight Moon.* New York: Harper, 1947.
A little bear says goodnight to each of the objects in the great green room.

Brunhoff, Jean de. *The Story of Babar.* New York: Random House, 1961.
The little elephant, Babar, meets the Old Lady and is elected King of the Elephants.

Bunting, Eve. *Butterfly House.* New York: Scholastic Press, 1999.
A little girl makes a house for a larva. Every spring after that butterflies come to visit her.

Burningham, John. *Mr. Gumpy's Motor Car.* New York: Crowell, 1976, 1973.
Mr. Gumpy's human and animal friends squash into his old car and go for a drive.

Campbell, Rod. *Dear Zoo.* New York: Four Winds Press, 1983.
Each animal arriving from the zoo as a possible pet fails to suit their prospective owner.

Cannon, Janell. *Stellaluna.* San Diego: Harcourt Brace Jovanovich, 1993.
A baby bat falls into a bird's nest, is raised as a bird, and is finely reunited with her mother.

Carle, Eric. *The Very Hungry Caterpillar.* New York: Philomel Books, 1987.
A little caterpillar eats his way through a varied quantity of food.

Carlson, Nancy. *I Like Me.* New York: Viking Kestrel, 1988.
By admiring her finer points, the narrator shows that she can take care of herself and have fun.

Crews, Donald. *Freight Train.* New York: Greenwillow Books, 1978.
The journey of a colorful train as it goes through tunnels, cities, and over trestles.

Cronin, Doreen. *Click Clack Moo: Cows Who Type.* New York: Simon and Schuster Books for Young Readers, 2000.
Farmer Brown's cows find a typewriter and start making demands.

Curtis, Jamie Lee. *Today I Feel Silly.* New York: HarperCollins Publishers, 1998.
A child's emotions range from silliness to anger to excitement, coloring and changing each day.

DePaola, Tomie. *Strega Nona.* New York: Simon and Schuster, 1975.
Strega Nona leaves her apprentice alone with her magic pasta pot.

DePaola, Tomie, *Tomie DePaola's Favorite Nursery Tales.* New York: Putnam, 1986.
An illustrated collection of traditional poems, fables, and stories.

Edwards, Pamela, *Some Smug Slug.* New York: HarperCollinsPublishers, 1996.
A smug slug that will not listen to the animals he meets and comes to an unexpected end.

Ehlert, Lois. *Color Farm.* New York: Lippincott, 1990.
The farm's rooster, dog, sheep, cow, pig, and other animals are colorful shapes.

Emberley, Ed. *Go away, Big Green Monster.* Boston: Little, Brown, 1992.
Bits of a monster are revealed and then disappear.

Falconer, Ian. *Olivia.* New York: Atheneum Books for Young Readers, 2000.
Olivia is a feisty pig who has too much energy for her own good.

Feiffer, Jules. *Bark, George.* New York: HarperCollins Publishers, 1999.
Instead of barking, George says, "meow", "quack", "oink", and "moo" until he is taken to the vet.

Fleming, Denis. *Lunch*. New York: Henry Holt and Co., 1992.
A very hungry mouse eats a large lunch comprised of colorful foods.

Fox, Mem. *Hattie the Fox*. New York: Bradbury Press, 1987, 1986.
Hattie, a hen, discovers a fox in the bushes creating various reactions, from other animals on the farm.

Freeman, Don. *Corduroy*. New York: Viking Press, 1968.
When a little girl buys a teddy bear, the bear finds what he has been searching for.

Gag, Wanda. *Millions of Cats*. New York: Coward, McCann, and Geoghegan, 1956.
The story of two peasants who go in search of one kitten and return with trillions of cats.

Galdone, Paul. *The Three Bears*. New York: Seabury Press, 1972.
Goldilocks finds the home of the Three Bears empty and roams at will.

Gliori, Debi. *No Matter What*. San Diego: Harcourt Brace, 1999.
Small, a little fox, seeks reassurance that Large will always provide love, no matter what.

Gollub, Matthew. *The Jazz Fly*. Santa Rosa, Calif.: Tortuga Press, 2000.
The Jazz Fly uses the rhymes he picks up on his way to town with his band.

Harper, Wilhelmina. *Gunniwolf*. New York: Dutton Children's Books, 2003.
A little girl wanders deep in the jungle and is confronted by the Gunniwolf.

Henkes, Kevin. *Julius, the Baby of the World*. New York: Greenwillow Books, 1990.
Lilly is convinced that the arrival of her new baby brother is the worst thing.

Hest, Amy. *In the Rain with Baby Duck*. Cambridge, Mass.: Candlewick Press, 1995.
Baby Duck does not like walking in the rain until Grandpa shares a secret with her.

Hoban, Tana. *So Many Circles, So Many Squares*. New York: Greenwillow Books, 1998.
The geometric concepts of circles and squares shown in photographs of familiar objects.

Hutchins, Pat. *Rosie's Walk*. New York: Macmillan, 1968.
Rosie the hen goes for a walk and never knew the fox was following her.

Irvine, Margaret. *Ella Sarah Gets Dressed*. San Diego: Harcourt, 2003.
Ella Sarah insists on wearing the striking and unusual outfit of her own choosing.

Johnson, Crockett. *Harold and the Purple Crayon*. New York: Harper and Row, 1955.
Walking in moonlight with his purple crayon, Harold creates many fantastic adventures.

Kasza, Keiko. *The Wolf's Chicken Stew*. New York: Putnam, 1987.
A hungry wolf's attempts to fatten a chicken for his stewpot have unexpected results.

Kellogg, Steven. *A-Hunting We Will Go*. New York: Morrow Junior Books, 1998.
Preparations for bedtime include, "A-reading we will go" and "Now off to bed we go!"

Kraus, Robert. *Leo the Late Bloomer*. New York: Windmill Books, 1971.
Leo, a young tiger, finally blooms under the anxious eyes of his parents.

Krauss, Ruth. *The Carrot Seed*. New York: Harper and Brothers, 1945.
A young boy knows that his carrot seed will come up.

Leaf, Munro. *The Story of Ferdinand*. New York: The Viking Press, 1936.
The story of a bull that would rather sit quietly under a tree than fight.

Lionni, Leo. *Little Blue and Little Yellow.* London: Hodder and Stoughton, 1962.
  A story of two colors that were such close friends they turned green.

London, Jonathan. *Froggy Gets Dressed.* New York: Viking, 1992.
  Rambunctious Froggy hops into snow forgetting to put on necessary articles of clothing.

McCloskey, Robert. *Make Way for Ducklings.* New York: Viking Press, 1941.
  Mr. and Mrs. Mallard take their babies to the pond in the Boston Public Garden.

McDermott, Gerald. *Anansi the Spider, a Tale from the Ashanti.* New York: Holt, Rinehart and Winston, 1972.
  On a long journey Anansi the Spider is saved by his sons; but which one to reward?

McMullan, Kate. *I Stink!* New York: Joanne Cotler Books, 2002.
  A big city garbage truck makes its rounds, consuming everything from apples to zucchini.

Marshall, James. *George and Martha.* Boston: Houghton Mifflin, 1972.
  Relates several episodes in the friendship of two hippopotamuses.

Martin, Bill. *Brown Bear, Brown Bear What Do You See?* New York: Henry Holt and Co., 1983.
  Children see a variety of animals, each a different color, and a teacher looking at them.

Mayer, Mercer. *There's a Nightmare in My Closet.* New York: Dial Press, 1968.
  A young boy decides to fight the nightmare in his closet.

Meddaugh, Susan. *Martha Blah Blah.* Boston: Houghton Mifflin, 1996.
  Missing letters in cans of soup calls for action by Martha, the talking dog.

Morales, Yuyi. *Just a Minute: A Trickster Tale and Counting Book.* San Francisco: Chronicle Books, 2003.
  Grandma Beetle is too busy making preparations for her birthday party to go with Senor Calaveras.

Mosel, Arlene. *Tikki Tikki Tembo.* New York: Holt, Rinehart and Winston, 1968.
  A folktale about why the Chinese came to give all their children short names.

My Very First Mother Goose. Cambridge, Mass.: Candlewick Press, 1996.
  A collection of more than sixty nursery rhymes.

Numeroff, Laura. *If You Give a Mouse A Cookie.* New York: Harper and Row, 1985.
  Requests by a mouse for a cookie take the mouse through a young child's day.

Piper, Watty. *The Little Engine That Could.* New York: Dutton Children's Books, 1998.
  It is the will of the little blue engine that gets the train to the other side of the mountain.

Polacco, Patricia. *Mr. Lincoln's Way.* New York: Philomel Books, 2001.
  Mr. Lincoln, the cool principal, helps Eugene overcome his intolerance.

Potter, Beatrix, *The Tale of Peter Rabbit.* New York: Little Simon, 1986.
  Peter disobeys his mother by going into Mr. McGregor's garden and almost gets caught.

Raffi. *Wheels on the Bus.* New York: Crown, 1988.
  Join in with the sounds of the bus and motions of the driver and passengers.

Rathmann, Peggy. *Good Night, Gorilla.* New York: Putnam, 1994.
  All the animals he left behind in the zoo follow an unobservant zookeeper home.

Rey, H. A. *Curious George Rides a Bike.* Boston: Houghton Mifflin, 1980.
   The adventures of George, the curious monkey, on his new bicycle.

Reynolds, Peter. *The Dot.* Cambridge, Mass.: Candlewick Press, 2003.
   Encouraged by her art teacher, Vashti changes her mind about being able to draw.

Rosen, Michael. *We're Going on a Bear Hunt.* New York: Margaret K. McElderry Books, 1989.
   Brave bear hunters go through grass, a river, mud, and other obstacles to meet a bear.

Schieszka, John. *The True Story of the Three Little Pigs by A. Wolf.* New York: Viking, 1989.
   The wolf gives his outlandish version of what really happened when he visited the pigs.

Sendak, Maurice, *Where the Wild Things Are.* New York: Harper and Row, 1963.
   Max is sent to bed for misbehaving; but escapes into an imaginary land full of monsters.

Seuss, Dr. *Horton Hatches the Egg.* New York: Random House, 1968, 1940.
   Through all sorts of hazards, Horton the elephant is rewarded for sitting on an egg.

Shaw, Nancy. *Sheep in a Jeep.* Boston: Houghton Mifflin, 1986.
   The misadventures of a group of sheep who go riding in a jeep.

Slobokina, Esphyr. *Caps for Sale.* New York: W. R. Scott, 1947.
   Mischievous monkeys steal every one of a peddler's caps while he naps under a tree.

Steig, William. *Sylvester and the Magic Pebble.* New York: Windmill Books, 1969.
   Sylvester the donkey asks his magic pebble to turn him into a rock.

Stocke, Janet. *Minerva Louise and the Red Truck.* New York: Dutton Children's Books, 2002.
   Minerva Louise loves playing in the red truck when one day the truck begins to move and she see many wonderful new things

Taback, Simms. *Joseph had a Little Overcoat.* New York: Viking, 1999.
   A very old overcoat is recycled numerous times into a variety of garments.

Tafuri, Nancy. *I Love You, Little One.* New York: Scholastic Press, 1998.
   Mama animals tell their little ones all the ways they are loved, forever and always.

Teague, Mark. *Dear Mrs. La Rue, Letters from Obedience School.* New York: Scholastic, 2002.
   Typewritten and paw-written letters beg Ike's owner to let him quit obedience school.

Van Allsburg, Chris. *Polar Express.* Boston: Houghton Mifflin, 1985.
   A magical train ride on Christmas Eve takes a boy to the North Pole to receive a gift.

Waddle, Martin. *Farmer Duck.* Boston: Candlewick Press, 1992.
   A lazy farmer is chased out of town by farm animals when a kind-hearted duck is overworked.

Walsh, Ellen Stoll. *Mouse Paint.* San Diego: Harcourt Brace Jovanovich, 1989.
   The adventure of three white mice who discover jars of red, blue, and yellow paint and some white paper.

Wells, Rosemary. *Noisy Nora.* New York: Dial Books for Young Readers, 1997.
   Nora makes more and more noise to attract her parents' attention.

Westcott, Nadine. *I Know an Old Lady Who Swallowed A Fly.* Boston: Little Brown, 1980.
   The solution proves worse than the predicament when an old lady swallows a fly.

Willems, Mo. *Don't Let the Pigeon Drive the Bus.* New York: Hyperion Books for Children, 2003.
When the bus drivers takes a break, a pigeon see a chance to drive the bus.

Williams, Linda. *The Little Old Lady Who Was Not Afraid of Anything.* New York: Crowell, 1986.
A little old lady who is not afraid of anything must deal with spooky objects.

Yolen, Jane. *How Do Dinosaurs Say Good Night?* New York: Blue Sky Press, 2000.
Mother and child ponder the different ways a dinosaur can say goodnight.

Zelinsky, Margot, *It Could Always Be Worse: A Yiddish Folktale.* New York: Farrar, Straus and Giroux, 1976.
Unable to stand his overcrowded and noisy home, a poor man goes to the rabbi for advice.

Zion, Gene, *Harry the Dirty Dog.* New York: HarperCollins, 1984.
Hating baths, a little dog hides his scrubbing brush, runs away from home and becomes a black dog with white spots that even his family doesn't recognize.

Appendix B

Finger Plays and Songs

Welcoming Songs, Alphabet Songs, Favorite Finger Plays, and Closing Songs

Hello Everybody

Hello everybody, how d'ya do,
How d'ya do, how d'ya do?
Hello everybody, how d'ya do,
How are you today?
Hello everybody, clap your hands,
Clap your hands, clap your hands.
Hello everybody, clap your hands,
How are you today?
(Repeat as above, using touch your nose, touch
    your toes, etc.)

The More We Get Together

The more we get together, together, together
The more we get together
The happier we'll be.
Cause your friends are my friends
And my friends are your friends
The more we get together
The happier we'll be.

If You're Ready For a Story (Tune: If You're Happy and You Know It)

If you're ready for a story, take a seat
If you're ready for a story, take a seat
Clap your hands and then your feet
Clap your hands and then your feet
 If you're ready for a story, take a seat

Good Morning Song
(Tune: "Where is Thumbkin?")

Good Morning, Good Morning
How are you?
How are you?

I'm so glad to see you
I'm so glad to see you
Teddy is too
Teddy is too. (Teddy is a puppet)

Right Hand, Left Hand

This is my right hand,
I'll raise it up high. *(Raise right hand.)*
This is my left hand,
I'll touch the sky. *(Raise left hand.)*
Right hand, *(Show right palm.)*
Left hand, *(Show left palm.)*
Roll them around. *(Roll hands around.)*
Left hand, *(Show left palm.)*
Right hand, *(Show right palm.)*
Pound, pound, pound. *(Pound fists together.)*

ABC Dance

(Have the group get into a circle and join hands,
and start walking clockwise as you sing
    "ABCDEFG."
Stop and go in the opposite direction (counter
    clockwise) singing "HIJKLMNOP."
Stop, move to the center of the circle with hands
    raised singing "QRS."
Move back out of the center singing "TUV."
Walk in clockwise singing
"WXY and Z. Now I know my ABCs, won't you
    sing along with me?")

Five Little Ducks

Five little ducks went to play
(hold up five fingers on right hand)
Over the hills and far away.

From *Building Blocks: Building a Parent-Child Early Literacy Program at Your Library* by Sharon Snow. Westport, CT: Libraries Unlimited. Copyright © 2007 by Sharon Snow.

(move hand in a waving motion and hide behind
   your back)
Mamma Duck, called "quack, quack, quack."
(move fingers of left hand to touch thumb, like a
   beak)
Only four little ducks came back.
(bring hand from behind back with only four
   fingers up)
(Repeat, losing one duck each time until you are
   left with no ducks, then father duck with left
   hand calls)
"Quack, quack, quack"
And five little ducks came back.

Grandma's Glasses

These are Grandma's glasses
(make glasses with fingers)
This is Grandpa's hat
(tap head)
This is how he folds his hands,
(fold hands)
And puts them in his lap.
(place hands in lap)

Here Is A Beehive

Here is a beehive
(make a beehive with fists)
Where are the bees?
(pretend to look around for them)
Watch, here they come
(open up the fist and hold up fingers one at a
   time)
One, two three, four, five
Buzzzzzzzzzz, buzzzzzzzz.

Hickory, Dickory, Dock

Hickory, dickory, dock.
(stand, swing arm like pendulum)
The mouse ran up the clock.
(run hand up arm)
The clock struck one.
(clap hands over head once)
The mouse ran down.
(run hand down arm)
Hickory, dickey, dock.
(stand, swing arm like pendulum)

I Wiggle

I wiggle, wiggle, wiggle, my fingers.
(wiggle fingers)

I wiggle, wiggle, wiggle my toes.
(wiggle toes)
I wiggle, wiggle, wiggle my shoulders.
(wiggle shoulders)
I wiggle, wiggle, wiggle, my nose.
(wiggle nose)
Now no more wiggles are left in me.
(shake head)
I am sitting as still as still can be.
(sit still)

Wheels on the Bus

The wheels on the bus go round and round,
   round and round, round and round
The wheels on the bus go round and round
All through the town.
The wipers on the bus go swish, swish, swish,
swish, swish, swish, swish, swish
The wipers on the bus go swish, swish, swish
All through the town.
*[Verses about the window, the doors, the baby and the
   mommy can be added ending with the horn]*
The horn on the bus goes beep, beep, beep, beep,
   beep, beep
Beep, beep, beep
The horn on the bus goes beep, beep, beep
All throught the town.

If You're Happy and You Know It

If you're happy and you know it, clap your
   hands.
(clap hands twice)
If you're happy and you know it, clap your
   hands.
(clap hands twice)
If you're happy and you know it, then your face
   will surely
show it.
(point to face)
If you're happy and you know it, clap your hands.
(clap hands twice)
If you're happy and you know it, stomp your
   feet.
If you're happy and you know it, (stomp feet
   twice), etc.
If you're happy and you know it then you're face
   will surely show it
(point to face)
If you're happy and you know it stomp
   your feet.
If you're happy and you know it, shout "hurray!"

(hurray!)
 If you're happy and you know it shout "hurray!"
(hurray!)
If you're happy and you know it then you're face
    will surely show it
(point to face)
If you're happy and you know it shout "hurray!"
If you're happy and you know it do all three
(clap hands, stomp feet, and shout hurray!)
If you're happy and you know it do all three
(clap hand, stomp feet, and shout hurray!)
If you're happy and you know it than your face
    will surely show it.
If you're happy and you know it do all three.

My Bonnie Lies Over the Ocean

My Bonnie (raise hands over head) lies over the
    ocean.
My Bonnie (put hands down) lies over the
    ocean.
My Bonnie (raise hands over head) lies over the
    ocean.
Please bring back my Bonnie (put hands down)
    to me.
Chorus:
Bring (raise hands) back (put hands down).
Bring. (raise hands) back (put hands down).
Oh, bring (raise hands) back (put hands down).
My Bonnie (raise hands) to me, to me.
Bring (put hands down) back (put hands down).
Bring (raise hands) back (put hands down).
Oh, bring (raise hands) back my Bonnie
    (put hands down) to me, to me.

Row, Row, Row Your Boat

Row, row, row your boat
Gently down the stream.
Merrily, merrily, merrily, merrily,
Life is but a dream.

Teddy Bear, Teddy Bear

Teddy Bear, Teddy Bear.
Touch the sky
Teddy Bear, Teddy Bear touch your toes.
(touch your toes)
Teddy Bear, Teddy Bear.
Turn around.
(turn around in a circle)
Teddy Bear, Teddy Bear.
Sit right down.

Ten Little Fingers

I have ten little fingers.
(hold up ten fingers)
And they all belong to me.
(point to self)
I can make them do things.
(wiggle fingers) Do you want to see?
(tilt head)
I can shut them up tight
(close finger up tight making a fist)
I can open them up wide
(open up fingers and hold them out in front
    of you)
I can put them together
(fold hands together)
I can make them hide
(hide them behind your back)
I can hold them up high
(open up hand and hold them up high)
I can hold them down low.
(hold hands down to ground)
I can fold them together just so.
(fold hands together)

Where is Thumbkin?

(hands behind back)
Where is thumbkin?
Where is thumbkin?
Here I am. Here I am.
(bring out right thumb, then left)
How are you today, sir?
(bend right thumb)
Very well, I thank you.
(bend left thumb)
Run away. Run away.
(put right thumb behind back, then
left thumb behind back.)
Other verses:
Where is Pointer?
Where is Middle Man?
Where is Ring Man?
Where is Pinky?
Where are all of them?

Good-bye Rhyme

Our hands say thank you with a clap, clap, clap
Our feet say thank you with a tap, tap, tap
Clap, clap, clap,
Tap, tap, tap
We roll our hands around and
We say good-bye (wave)

Now it's time to say Good-bye
(Tune: "London Bridge")

Now it's time to say good-bye,
Say goodbye, say good-bye,
Now it's time to say good-bye,
I'll see you all next time.

The Farmer's in the Dell

The Farmer's in the Dell
The Farmer's in the Dell
Heigh-Ho My Derry-O
The Farmer takes a wife
The Farmer takes a wife
Heigh-Ho My Derry-O
The Wife takes a child, etc.
The Child takes a mouse, etc.
The Mouse takes the cheese, etc.
The Cheese stands alone

Hokey Pokey

You put your left hand in
You put your left hand out
You put your left hand in
And you shake it all about
You do the Hokey Pokey and you turn yourself
   around
And that's what it's all about.
(clap hands)
You put your right hand in, etc.
You put your left leg in, etc.
You put your right leg in, etc.
You put your whole self in, etc.

Say and Touch

Say pup; now stand up!
Say laugh; now touch your calf!
Say bee; now touch your knee.
Say paste; now touch your waist.
Say yummy; now touch your tummy.
Say colder; now touch your shoulder.
Say sand; now touch your hand.
Say clown; and now sit down!

Come Along Everyone

Come along, come along, come along everyone
Come along everyone, sit on the floor
Not on the ceiling, not on the door
Come along everyone sit on the floor

Five Little Monkeys Jumping
on the Bed

Five little monkeys jumping on the bed.
One fell off and bumped his head.
Mamma called the doctor, and the
   doctor said,
"No more monkeys jumping on the bed."
(repeat, subtracting a monkey each time)

ABC Song

A-B-C-D-E-F-G
H-I-J-K-L-M-N-O-P
Q-R-S-T-U-and V,
W-X-Y and Z.
Now I know my ABC's
Next time won't you sing with me?

Appendix C

Home Literacy Environment Checklist

The complete version of this checklist is available from http://www.wiu.edu/ itlc/ws/ws2/litenv_3.php. A sample of the questions are shown below:

What my child has. . .

> at least one alphabet book (e.g., Dr. Seuss's *ABC book*).
> magnetized alphabet letters to play with.

What I or another adult in the house do. . .

> read a picture books with my child at least once a week.
> teach new words to my child at least once a week.

What my child sees me or another adult in the house doing. . .

> reading books, magazines, or the newspaper at least once a week.

Now or in the past, I or another adult in the house encourage or help my child. . .

> to watch beginning reading shows on TV or tapes.

Appendix D

Print Awareness and Print Motivation

Finger Plays, Songs, and Activities

Purpose: To reinforce print awareness and print motivation skills.

Twinkle, Twinkle Traffic Light (author unknown, sung to Twinkle, Twinkle Little Star)

Twinkle, twinkle traffic light, (hold up hands and open and shut them)
Shining on the corner bright, (continue to open and shut hands)
Red means stop, (hold hand up like stop)
Green means go, (point forward)
Yellow means just go slow, (creep pointer and middle fingers on other hand very slowly)
Twinkle, twinkle traffic light, (hold up hands and open and shut them)
Shining on the corner bright. (continue to open and shut hands)

Stop/Go (by Texas State Library)

Standing on the sidewalk, (stand)
Need to cross the street.
Waiting for the green light, (open and shut hands, like a light)
Before I can move my feet.
I can see the red light.
Red means STOP! (hold hand up like a stop)
When I see the green light,
I can walk, skip, hop! (hop up and down)

The Thing (author unknown)

I got a lot of paper, (hold out hands flat)
I got a lot of string.
I tied it all together (pretend to tie something up)
And made a special thing.
I got a lot of markers,

I wrote a lot of words, (act like you're writing)
I drew a lot of pictures
Of elephants and birds. (swing arm like an elephant and flap wings like a bird)
I showed it to my neighbor,
I showed it to my dad, (make a motion with your hand to show height)
But no one ever figured out
Exactly what I had. (shrug shoulders)
I showed it to the baby,
I let her have a look. (make a binocular with your hands and act like you're looking at something)
She chewed upon the pages.
She knew it was a book! (hold hands out flat)

Picture People: (*Ring a Ring O' Roses* by Flint Public Library)

I like to peek inside a book (hold hands out flat)
Where all the picture people look. (shade eyes, act like you're looking at something)
I like to peek at them and see (continue looking)
If they are peeking back at me. (continue looking, but this time, look around too)

The Library (author unknown)

This is the library (open arms wide)
Here is a book (hold hands flat
Open it up (open hands out, palms up)
And take a look (shade eyes, act like you're looking at something)

From *Building Blocks: Building a Parent-Child Early Literacy Program at Your Library* by Sharon Snow. Westport, CT: Libraries Unlimited. Copyright © 2007 by Sharon Snow.

Appendix E

Print Motivation Bibliography

Carle, Eric. *The Secret Birthday Message.* New York: Crowell, 1972.
  By following the instructions in the coded message, Tim finds his birthday present.

Ehlert, Lois. *Pie in the Sky.* Orlando, Fla.: Harcourt, 2004.
  A father and child watch the cherry tree in their backyard, waiting until there are ripe cherries to bake in a pie.

Faulkner, Keith. *Pop! Went Another Balloon.* New York: Dutton, 2002.
  Toby is on his way to Tina's house with a bunch of colorful balloons. Watch as they magically disappear with each turn of the page.

Lloyd, Sam. *What Color is Your Underwear?* New York: Scholastic, 2004.
  A lift-the-flap book that takes a peek at the color of different animal's underwear.

Steer, Donald. *Snappy Little Opposites.* Brookfield, Conn.: Millbrook Press, 2000.
  Big or small? In or out? Awake or asleep? This book has captivating animal characters, lively rhymes, and 10 big pop-ups.

Steiner, Joann. *Look-Alike Jr.* Boston: Little Brown, 1999.
  Simple verses challenge readers to identify everyday objects used to construct 11 different three-dimensional scenes, including a house, kitchen, bedroom, school bus, train, farm, and rocket.

  See other great books by these authors.

Appendix F

Non-Fiction (Informational) Bibliography

Allen, Judy. *Are You a Butterfly?* (Backyard Books Series): New York: Kingfisher, 2000.

Bingham, Caroline. *Big Book of Trucks.* New York: DK Publishing, 1999.

C is for Construction: Big Trucks and Diggers from A to Z. San Francisco, Calif.: Chronicle Books, 2003.

Cooper, John. *Dinosaurs* (Scary Creatures Series). New York: Watts, 2002.

Daly, Kathleen. *Big Golden Book of Backyard Birds.* Racine, Wis.: Western Publishing Co., 1990.

Darling, Kathy. *ABC Dogs.* New York: Walker and Co, 1997.

Davis, Kelly. *See-Through Pirates.* Philadelphia, Penn.: Running Press Kids, 2003.

Dewan, Ted. *Inside Dinosaurs and Other Prehistoric Creatures.* New York: Delacorte Press, 1994.

Dodson, Peter. *An Alphabet of Dinosaurs.* New York: Scholastic, 1995.

Greenaway, Theresa. *Big Book of Bugs.* New York: Dorling Kindersley, 2000.

Harrison, Michael *New Oxford Treasury of Children's Poems.* Oxford, N.Y.: Oxford Press, 1995.

Hoberman, Mary Ann. *You Read to Me, I'll Read to You.* New York: Little Brown, 2005.

Kirk, Daniel. *Go!* New York: Hyperion Books for Children, 2001.

Legg, Gerald. *World of Insect Life,* (Inside Look Series). Milwaukee, Wis.: Garth Stevens Publishers, 2002.

Lillegard, Dee. *Wake Up House!* New York: Knopf, 2004.

Macquitty, Miranda. *Sharks* (Eyewitness Series*).* London: DK Publishing, 2004.

Parsons, Alexandra. *Amazing Spiders* (Eyewitness Junior Series). New York: Knopf, 1990.

Parsons, Alexandra. *Planes* (What's Inside? Series). New York: Doris Kinddersley, 1992.

Pipe, Jim. *The Giant Book of Sharks & Other Scary Predators.* Broofield, Conn.: Cooper Beech Books, 1999.

Platt, Richard. *Incredible Body.* New York: DK Publishing, 1998.

Press, Judy. *Little Hands Art Book.* Charlotte, Vt.: Williamson Publishers, 1994.

Robertson, Matthew. *Insects and Spiders* (Reader's Digest Pathfinders). Pleasantville, N.Y.: Reader's Digest Children's Publications, 2000.

Stetson, Emily, *Little Hands Fingerplays & Action Songs.* Charlotte, Vt.: Williamson Publishers, 2001.

Stille, Darlene. *Freight Trains.* Minneapolis, Minn.: Compass Point Books, 2002.

Stille, Darlene. *Fire Trucks.* Minneapolis, Minn.: Compass Point Books, 2003.

Torres, Laura. *Ten-Minute Crafts for Preschoolers.* New York: Disney Press, 2000.

Appendix G

Reading Readiness for Preschool Parents

Finger Plays, Songs, and Activities

Twinkle, Twinkle Traffic Light (author unknown, sung to Twinkle, Twinkle Little Star)

Twinkle, twinkle traffic light, (hold up hands and open and shut them)
Shining on the corner bright, (continue to open and shut hands)
Red means stop, (hold hand up like stop)
Green means go, (point forward)
Yellow means just go slow, (creep pointer and middle fingers on other hand very slowly)
Twinkle, twinkle traffic light, (hold up hands and open and shut them)
Shining on the corner bright. (continue to open and shut hands)

Stop/Go (by Texas State Library)

Standing on the sidewalk, (stand)
Need to cross the street.
Waiting for the green light, (open and shut hands, like a light)
Before I can move my feet.
I can see the red light.
Red means STOP! (hold hand up like a stop)
When I see the green light,
I can walk, skip, hop! (hop up and down)

The Thing (author unknown)

I got a lot of paper, (hold out hands flat)
I got a lot of string.
I tied it all together, (pretend to tie something up)
And made a special thing.
I got a lot of markers,
I wrote a lot of words. (act like you're writing)

I drew a lot of pictures
Of elephants and birds. (swing arm like an elephant trunk and flap wings like a bird)
I showed it to my neighbor,
I showed it to my dad, (make a motion with your hand to show height)
But no one ever figured out
Exactly what I had. (shrug shoulders)
I showed it to the baby,
I let her have a look. (make a binocular with your hands and act like you're looking at something)
She chewed upon the pages.
She knew it was a book! (hold hands out flat)

Picture People (Ring a Ring O' Roses by Flint Public Library)

I like to peek inside a book (hold hands out flat)
Where all the picture people look. (shade eyes, act like you're looking at something)
I like to peek at them and see (continue looking)
If they are peeking back at me.
(continue looking, but this time, look around too)

Appendix H

Letter Sounds for Letter Day Activities

To develop vocabulary, do finger plays that describe new words in a fun, rhythmic way!

ABC Song
A-B-C-D-E-F-G
H-I-J-K-L-M-N-O-P
Q-R-S-T-U-and V,
W-X-Y and Z.
Now I know my ABC's
Next time won't you sing with me?
Alternatives include singing in different voices:
   monster, baby, and so on.

BINGO (author unknown)
There was a farmer who had a dog,
And Bingo was his name-o.
B-I-N-G-O (3 times)
And Bingo was his name-o.
There was a farmer who had a dog,
And Bingo was his name-o.
(clap)-I-N-G-O (3 times)
And Bingo was his name-o.
There was a farmer who had a dog,
And Bingo was his name-o.
(clap)-(clap)-N-G-O (3 times)
And Bingo was his name-o.
There was a farmer who had a dog,
And Bingo was his name-o.
(clap)-(clap)-(clap)-G-O (3 times)
And Bingo was his name-o.
There was a farmer who had a dog,
And Bingo was his name-o.
(clap)-(clap)-(clap)-(clap)-O (3 times)
And Bingo was his name-o.
There was a farmer who had a dog,

And Bingo was his name-o.
(clap)-(clap)-(clap)-(clap)-(clap) (3 times)
And Bingo was his name-o.

ABCD Dinosaur (author unknown, sung to the tune of Twinkle, Twinkle, Little Star)
ABCD Dinosaur
That is what the D stands for
Some are big and some are small
I like dinosaurs most of all
ABCD Dinosaur
That is what the D stands for

My Tricycle (author unknown)
I have a tricycle with wheels so fine,
One in front and two behind, (point)
I steer from left to right, (act like steering)
I peddle so fast, I'm out of sight! (pump legs up
   and down)

Here Comes the Choo Choo Train (author unknown)
Here comes the choo choo train,
Puffing up the track, (move arms like a train)
Now its going forward, (lean forward)
Now its going back, (lean backward)
Hear the bell as it rings, (shake hand like bell)
Now hear the whistle blow, (whistle)
What a lot of noise it makes, (cover ears)
Everywhere it goes!

Itsy Bitsy Spider (author unknown)

The itsy bitsy spider,
Went up the water spout, (pointer fingers and
    thumbs touch to creep up)
Down came the rain, (bring hands down
    like rain)

And washed the spider out, (hands apart)
Out came the sun (arms make arc above head)
To dry up all the rain,
And the itsy bitsy spider,
Went up the spout again. (pointer fingers and
    thumbs touch to creep up

Appendix I
Vocabulary Bibliography

Baker, Alan, *Little Rabbit's First Word Book.* New York: Kingfisher, 1996.
Rabbits present words and matching pictures grouped under such topics as toys, food, things that move, animals, and drawing and painting. Includes simple word and concept games.

Crews, Donald. *Freight Train.* New York: Greenwillow 1978.
A freight train is described with words about transportation, geography, and color in a simple and attractive book.

Fleming, Denise. *The Everything Book.* New York: Henry Holt, 2000.
The world around us in pictures and verse.

Henkes, Kevin. *Owen.* New York: Greenwillow, 1993.
There is a wealth of verbs and adjectives in this story of growing up.

Martin, Bill, Jr. *Panda Bear, Panda Bear, What do you see?* New York: Henry H. Holt, 1991.
Discover the world of animals with Panda Bear.

Wood, Audrey. *The Napping House.* San Diego: Harcourt, 1984.
Naptime turns into silliness—with lots of fun and interesting new words.

Scholastic Visual Dictionary. New York: Scholastic, 2000.
This dictionary stands out because of its beautiful pictures and thematic organization.

See other great books by these authors!

Appendix J

Vocabulary

Aliki. *All by Myself!* New York: HarperCollins Publisher, 2000.
   A boy shows all the steps he takes to get dressed, eat, go to school, play, and get ready for bed.

Ballard, Robin. *My Day, Your Day.* New York: Greenwillow Books, 2001.
   Some people spend their days at school, and some spend their days at work. surprisingly similar.

Forward, Toby. *What Did You Do Today: The First Day of School.* New York: Clarion Books, 2004.
   A child describes the first day of school, from making sandwiches for lunch to holding a parent's hand on the walk home.

Harper, Jessica. *Lizzy's Ups and Downs: Not an Ordinary School Day.* New York: HarperCollins, 2004.
   Ask someone how his day went, and maybe it will be as crazy as Lizzy's.

Kroninger, Stephen. *If I Crossed the Road.* New York: Atheneum Books for Young Readers, 1997.
   A young boy imagines all the fantastic things that he might do, if only his mother would let him cross the road.

Rosen, Michael. *We're Going on a Bear Hunt.* New York: Margaret K. McElderry Books, 1989.
   Brave bear hunters go through grass, a river, mud, and other obstacles before the inevitable encounter with the bear forces a headlong retreat.

   See more great books by these authors.

Appendix K
Children's Dictionaries

American Heritage. *My Very Own Big Dictionary*. Boston: Houghton Mifflin, 1994.
  Contains everyday words in alphabetical order with illustrations of activity-filled scenes. Contains suggestions for additional language activities.

American Heritage Picture Dictionary. Boston: Houghton Mifflin, 2006.
  Introduces preschoolers and beginning reader to the idea of alphabetical organizations. Each word defined by a sentence using the word to describe the object or activity portrayed in the accompanying illustration.

Amery, Heather. *First Thousand Words in English*. Tulsa, Okla.: EDC, 2003.
  Detailed drawings introduce 1000 common words.

Baker, Alan. *Little Rabbit's First Word Book*. New York: Kingfisher, 1996.
  Rabbit presents words and matching pictures grouped under such topics as toys, food, colors, and shapes.

DK Ultimate Visual Dictionary. New York: DK Press, 2002.
  Explains the world with a unique marriage of words and picture. A treasure trove of knowledge.

Feldman, Thea. *Disney Picture Dictionary*. New York: Disney Press, 2003.
  A dictionary of words and their meanings to help preschoolers and young grade-schoolers develop language, spelling and vocabulary skills.

Priddy, Roger. *My Fun Picture Dictionary*. New York: Holtzbrinck Publishers, 2003.
  A dictionary of words relevant to daily life and words children need to know at the preschool age. Helps children learn new words daily.

Seuss, Dr. *Cat in the Hat Beginning Book Dictionary*. New York: Random House Books for Young Readers, 1964.
  A wacky cast of characters reappears throughout the dictionary which pairs words with pictures that carry their meaning, making it simple enough even for nonreaders to understand. This is perhaps the only dictionary in the world that is fun to read!

Taback, Simms. *Simms Taback's Big Book of Words*. Maplewood, N.J.: Big Apple Books, 2004.
  Labeled illustrations are grouped under play things, clothing, food and music.

From *Building Blocks: Building a Parent-Child Early Literacy Program at Your Library* by Sharon Snow. Westport, CT: Libraries Unlimited. Copyright © 2007 by Sharon Snow.

Appendix L

Narrative Bibliography

Agee, Jon. *Why Did the Chicken Cross the Road?* New York: Dial Books for Young Readers, 2006.
Fourteen illustrators have answered this question in their own way. Each illustrator makes up a story from their illustrations to tell why the chicken crossed the road.

Chodos-Irvine, Margaret. *Ella Sarah Gets Dressed.* San Diego: Harcourt, 2003.
Despite the advice of others in her family, Ella Sarah persists in wearing the striking and unusual outfit of her own choosing.

Kazka, Keiko. *Wolf's Chicken Stew.* New York: Putnam, 1987.
A hungry wolf's attempt to fatten a chicken for his stewpot has unexpected results.

Nevius, Carol. *Karate Hour.* New York: Marshall Cavenish, 2004.
Rhyming text portrays the exuberance of an hour of karate class.

Numeroff, Laura. *If You Give a Mouse a Cookie.* New York: Harper and Row, 1998.
Relating the cycle of requests a mouse is likely to make after you give him a cookie takes the reader through a young child's day.

Rosen, Michael. *We're Going on a Bear Hunt.* New York: Margaret K.: McElderry Books, 1989.
Brave bear hunters go through grass, a river, mud, and other obstacles before the inevitable encounter with the bear forces a headlong retreat.

Taback, Simms. *Joseph Had a Little Overcoat.* New York: Viking, 1999.
A very old overcoat is recycled numerous times into a variety of garments

Willems, Mo. *Knuffle Bunny: A Cautionary Tale.* New York: Hyperion Books for Children, 2004.
A trip to the Laundromat leads to a momentous occasion when Trixie, who is too young to speak words, realizes that something important is missing and struggles to explain the problem to her father.

See more great books by these authors.

Appendix M

Phonological Awareness Bibliography

Books

Aylesworth, Jim. *Old Black Fly.* New York: Holt, 1992.
  Rhyming text and illustrations follow a mischievous old black fly through the alphabet as he has a very busy bad day landing where he should not be.

Beaumont, Karen. *I Ain't Going to Paint No More.*
  In the rhythm of a familiar folk song, a child cannot resist adding one more dab of paint in surprising places.

Degan, Bruce. *Jamberry.* New York: Harper Row, 1983.
  A little boy walking in the forest meets a big, lovable bear that takes him on a delicious berry-picking adventure in the magical world of Berryland.

Lewis, Kevin. *My Truck Is Struck.* New York: Hyperion, 2002.
  When a dump truck hauling a big load gets stuck in the mud, progressively larger vehicles try to pull it out.

Rex, Michael. *Dunk Skunk.* New York: G. P. Putnam's Sons, 2003.
  Sports actions rhyme with the names of animals who love to play, such as Goal Mole, Dunk Skunk, and Hurdle Turtle

Webb, Steve. *Tanka Tanka Skunk.* New York: Orchard, 2004.
  Uses animal names to introduce rhythmic language and rhyme, as Tanka the elephant and his friend, Skunk, play drums to keep the beat.

Wilson, Karma. *Bear Wants More.* New York: McElderry Books, 2003.
  When spring comes, Bear wakes up very hungry and is treated to great food by his friends.

  See other great books by these authors.

Finger Plays and Songs

To reinforce phonological awareness and narrative skills.

One Two, Buckle My Shoe (Mother Goose)

One, two, buckle my shoe,
Three, four, shut the door,
Five, six, pick up sticks,
Seven, eight, lay them straight,
Nine, ten, big fat hen.

Willoughby, Wallaby, Woo (author unknown)

Willoughby, wallaby, woo,
An elephant sat on you,
Willoughby, wallaby wames,
An elephant sat on James,
(Repeat with different names)

Five Fat Peas (author unknown)

Five fat peas in a pea pod pressed, (clasp both
    hands together in a fist)
One grew, two grew, (extend thumbs together
    and then extend index fingers together)
And so did all the rest, (continue extending
    fingers)
They grew and they grew, and they never
    stopped, (move hands apart slowly)
They grew so fat that the pea-pod POPPED! (clap
    hands on the word *popped*)

Flutter, Flutter, Butterfly (author unknown)

Flutter, flutter butterfly
Floating in the springtime sky
Floating by for all to see
Floating by so merrily
Flutter, flutter, butterfly
Floating in the springtime sky!
(act like a butterfly)

Little Rabbit Foo Foo (unknown author, this version from: http://friendsofeic.tripod.com/ hokey.html#Little Rabbit Foo-Foo)

Little Rabbit Foo Foo, hopping through the
    forest, (two fingers like bunny ears hop)
Scooping up the field mice, and bopping 'em on
    the head. (scoop with hand, then bop hand)
Along came the good fairy, and she said:
"Little Rabbit Foo Foo, I don't want to see you,
    scooping up the field mice, and bopping 'em
    on the head. (shake finger)

I'll give you three more chances, and then I'm
    gonna turn you into a goon!" (show three
    fingers)
(Repeat, until there are no more chances)
"… so I'm turning you into a goon! POOF!"
(The moral of the story is: Hare today, and Goon
    tomorrow.)

This Old Man (author unknown)

This old man, he played one, (hold up one finger)
He played knick knack on my thumb, (tap on
    thumb with other hand)
With a knick knack, paddy whack
Give a dog a bone, (pat lap in rhythm to the
    song)
This old man went rolling home (make rolling
    motions with hands)
(Repeat in numerical progression from: two-*shoe*,
    three-*knee*, four-*door*, five-*hive*, six-*sticks*,
    seven-*up to heaven*, eight-*gate*, nine-*line*,
    ten-*once again*)

Appendix N

Certificates

This is the wording that can be used for a certificate. You should add a border or use decorative paper. It is best to print in landscape.

READY TO READ

Presented to

_____

You are on your way to being a reader.

You have completed the
Every Child Ready to Read @ your library program
on

_____

_____
Signature of the Children's Presenter

_____
Signature of the Adult's Presenter

Signature of the Director, Branch Head
or Significant other persons

CONGRATULATIONS!

You have the skills to help your child be a reader.

You have completed the
Every Child Ready to Read @ your library

on

Index

About the Author

SHARON SNOW is the Young Adult Services Librarian at the Palm Springs Public Library in Palm Springs, California.